Sociology Revision & Test Yourself
AS-Level
Family, Education &
Research Methods

SOCIOLOGYTWYNHAM.COM

ACKNOWLEDGEMENT

Special thanks to pixabay.com for allowing the use of their image on the front cover.

CONTENTS REVISION SECTION

PLEASE NOTE

First and foremost this is a revision guide book designed to supplement rather than replace your text book. Test Yourself AS - Sociology books accompany this series and also are available from Amazon.

1 FAMILIES AND HOUSEHOLDS

Defining the family - the Office of National statistics defines the family as: "a married, civil partnered or cohabiting couple with or without children, or a lone parent with at least one child.

Types of families - there are several types of recognized family structures; blended/reconstituted family; extended family; gay or lesbian family; lone parent family; nuclear family; modified extended family; polygamous family; beanpole family and symmetrical family.

Defining a household- at its simplest a household consists of one person living alone or a group of people who share living arrangements at the same address for example a group of university students.

COMPETING PERSPECTIVES OF THE FAMILY (in other words different views on what the family is for)

There are different or competing perspectives on the family: Functionalist; Marxist; Feminist; New Right and Postmodern.

- **Functionalist perspective:** argues the family is a functional prerequisite as it plays the key role in maintaining social stability. Murdock examined 250 societies and found the family performs four basic functions:

    1. Sexual – the family provides stable sexual relationships for adults and controls the sexual habits of its members
    2. Reproduction – helps provide new members of society
    3. Socialization – teaches children the norms and values of society to keep society functioning
    4. Economic – pools resources for all family members to share

- For Parsons (1951) the function of the family has two basic functions:

    1. primary socialization of children – see page 4
    2. stabilisation of adult personalities – see page 4

- **Marxist perspective**: sees the family as a tool of capitalism.

- Engles argued the nuclear family solved the problem of inheritance of private property.

- Althusser (1971) a French Marxist, argued that in order for capitalism to survive people must be taught how to think and behave, and the family is one of the best mechanisms for doing this. This is because the family is seen to help maintain the dominant position of the ruling class by teaching family members to submit to authority.

- Contemporary Marxists like Zaretsky (1976) see the family as an aid to capitalism because:

  1. the capitalist system is built on the domestic labour of housewives who produce future workers
  2. at the same time, the family consumes the products of capitalism, which perpetuates the profits for the ruling-class

- **Feminist perspectives**: view the family as oppressing women. There are three feminist approaches:

- **Radical feminists**: focus squarely on patriarchy as the instrument of oppression (emasculation) within the home. This perspective is evident in the work of Bryson (1992) who sees the oppression of women by men (patriarchy) as universal. Delphy and Leonard (1992) argue it is men rather than capitalism who benefit the most from exploiting women and the family is central in maintaining this structure as:

  1. families are structured; in this structure men dominate while women and children are subordinate (very few families are matriarchal)
  2. man's position in the family is the dominant one he tends to make the final decision on family issues
  3. while women have paid employment outside the home, yet they still have to undertake household tasks – this is known as the dual burden
  4. while some women have paid employment outside the home yet still remain responsible for the majority of household tasks and care for children – this is known as the triple-shift

- **Marxist feminists**: argue women's oppression benefits capitalism. Benston (1972) argues capitalism benefits from a large army of women – an unpaid workforce - who are compliant and willing to do as they're told because women have been socialized to act this way and women rears future workers to think the same way.

- Both radical and Marxist feminists argue the abolition of the family is needed to end women's oppression.

- **Liberal feminists'**: argue is women's oppression can be overcome by:

  1. changing the socialization patterns of males and females
  2. improving legislation on equal pay; divorce etc.

- **New Right perspective:** very similar in principle to functionalists - are concerned about the decline of the nuclear family.

    1. John Redwood (1993) a Conservative MP argued the natural state is for two parents to look after their children. The breadwinner husband and homemaker-wife model is the best structure for self-reliance, reducing the likelihood of welfare dependency

    2. Easier access to divorce has increased the number of single parents who are too dependent on welfare for their livelihood

    3. Charles Murray argues a welfare dependency has created a dependency culture as individuals find welfare benefits far more tempting than finding work. Murray termed the work-shy as the underclass

    4. New Right argue social policies have helped increase family diversity in the form of reconstituted and lone parent families have undermined the traditional family

- **Postmodernist perspective:** position focuses on there no longer being a perfect type of family structure as families are fashioned a refashioned to meet changing social and cultural needs – think of same sex families.

    1. Postmodernists see family diversity as an expression of personal choice and lifestyle choice (a point which makes the New Right shudder)

    2. Judith Stacey (1990) argues the diversity of family types has established themselves to the extent there will never be one dominant type in Western society again

CHANGING FAMILY STRUCTURES OVER TIME

- Pre-Industrial Families (pre-industrial means before industrialization) had large numbers of children. Family life in the pre-industrial period was characterized by the dominance of a family-based economy where work is mostly agricultural.

- Classic extended family in pre-industrial society, kinship dominates and the multifunctional extended family is the normal family structure. This structure consisted of male head of the family, his wife and children and aging parents. This type of family structure was common in the pre-industrial period:

    1. together the family worked as a productive unit producing the things needed to sustain the family's survival

    2. kin relationship during this period is one of binding obligations where an individual's status was ascribed

    3. during the industrialization period the function (purpose) of the family was multifunctional: economic production; educational; political; *ascribed status*

- Industrialization (the period from the start of the industrial revolution) functionalists say industrialization changed the function of the family. Parsons argues the nuclear family best meets the needs of industrial society as it allows individuals to achieve status. In addition *Parsons* argues the family now had two essential functions to perform because the nuclear family becoming structurally isolated – the isolated nuclear family:

    1. primary socialization – children learning society's culture helping establish a value consensus
    2. stabilization of adult personalities via the sexual division of labour (instrumental & expressive roles)

The above was due to the isolated nuclear family being:

    1. free from binding obligations to wider kin
    2. able to be geographically and socially mobile

The above points show how the nuclear family fits with the needs of industrial society by being structured to move to where work is and by rewarding individual achievement – *achieved status*. Therefore Parsons is arguing industrialization changed the roles and status of individuals within the family.

This social change means institutions become specialized – structural differentiation. Structural differentiation meant the state via the National Health Service (NHS); compulsory education and welfare services took on many of the traditional functions of the family, leaving the family to specialize in its two essential functions of primary socialization and the stabilization of adult personalities.

Parsons 'then and now' approach to family change was brought into question by research based evidence from other sociologists: Willmott and Young; Laslett; Anderson; Oakley argue there was more variety in family forms than Parsons suggests, see below:

4

Name	How has industrialization changed the family?
Talcott Parsons	The isolated nuclear family: 1. Led to the isolation of the nuclear family away from their wider kin 2. Loss of traditional functions undertaken by classic extended family 3. Status now achieved (was ascribed) 4. Has become a mobile workforce
Peter Laslett	1. Found only 10% of households between 1564-1821 included kin (fitted classic extended model) 2. Laslett argues nuclear families were the norm in pre-industrial England
Michael Anderson	1. Argues the early stages of industrialization encouraged extended families 2. Anderson took a sample of homes in Preston and found the working class relied on families for support 3. Overcrowding was an issue as people shared homes to save rent
Women in Families – Ann Oakley	1. 1842 Mines Act – banned women from being miners 2. Around same time laws were passed preventing women being employed in industries 3. Above caused economic dependence of women on men 4. Above meant the isolation of housework and child care from being seen as 'work' 5. Women 'forced' to adopt mother/housewife as primary role

Willmott and Young
 	
Symmetrical family
	Identify four stages in the development of the family:
	
	1. Stage 1 (up to 1750) the pre - industrial family was a unit of economic production with the main family structure being nuclear
	2. Stage 2 (from 1750 to 1900) most working class families in industrial areas were extended families with an growing difference between work in the home and paid employment
	3. Stage 3 (from 1900) symmetrical family becomes the norm, with more family life centred around the home – *hence privatised nuclear family* - with:
	    • free time being devoted to chores and odd-jobs
	    • leisure is mainly home-based with increased TV usage
	    • strong conjugal bonds
	    • husband and wife relationships more about companionship by sharing experiences in and outside the home
	4. Stage 4 (the future) they predicted a family structure characterised by 'work-centred' individuals

Demographic trends also influence family structures

Other influences on family size are changing birth rates; increased life expectancy and improved infant mortality rates. These changes are largely due to:

1. advances in medicine, public hygiene and health education
2. welfare state (social security)
3. nutrition and diet
4. working conditions
5. rise of individualism

Social policies also influence family structures

Social policy refers to government legislation (laws on abortion; marriage; divorce etc) and activities (policies which shape education; health; taxation etc) which seek to improve the wellbeing of its people (as discussed above, social policies on childhood). Therefore politicians use legislation to influence family structures.

In 1945 The Welfare State was a social policy set up to allow the state to support families through:

- welfare benefits, housing, health-care and education

During 1960s and 1970s legislation helped influence family structure:

- the 1969 Divorce Reform Act made it easier for women to file for divorce which was seen to threaten the family by some politicians as it increased the number of families headed by women (a point which did not trouble feminists)

From 1979 the Conservative Government wanted to protect traditional family with

- Child Support Agency (CSA) – kept tabs on 'errant fathers'

- Children Act 1989 – gave children rights

From 1997 the New Labour Government recognized family diversity as well as marriage

- 'Supporting Families' consultation paper valued marriage for families

- yet their 2005 civil partnership legislation recognized the diversity of family structures

From 2010 the Conservative Government still values traditional family structures through:

- welfare policies which reduce individuals' dependency on the state (cutting benefit payments) and increases it on the family by making the family take care of the individuals within it such as an unemployed spouse by pooling resources instead of claiming welfare

Feminists argue the Conservatives and the New Right social policies seek to keep women in the home while New Labour might recognize family diversity but still support patriarchal society through social policies which keep women as primary carer.

An assessment of social policies from the competing perspectives:

New Right thinkers (popular with the Conservative Party) argue social policies should be designed to support the nuclear family. As the nuclear family is constructed on breadwinner/homemaker model, social policies need to encourage self-reliance which would reduce a culture of dependence identified by Charles Murray as being a cause of many social ills. Criticisms – feminists would point out it tries to force women back into subordinate role. It also assumes patriarchal nuclear family is 'natural' rather than socially constructed. Marxists would point out it would push more working-class families into poverty.

Marxists point out how social policies serve the ruling class at the expense of the working class. Althusser (1971) argued that in order for capitalism to survive people must be taught how to think and behave, and the family is one of the best mechanisms for doing this as it gets working-class parents to put their children through an education system which produces obedient and docile workers. Another example is the low level of state pension for workers too old to work are being 'sustained' at lowest possible cost.

However functionalists point out the purpose of social policies is the way they function/contribution they make towards social stability. Functionalists like Fletcher see social policy as an outcome of the march of progress towards a society where the family is assisted by the state rather than social policies being a form of state social control. Criticisms – feminists would point out it assumes all members of the family benefit from social policies. Marxists would point out it assumes there is a march of progress for everyone.

Feminists argue social policies are still constructed on the belief women and children are dependent on a male breadwinner and so the function (purpose) of social polices is to keep society patriarchal. For example women's maternity leave is much longer than men's paternity leave, the assumption being women will automatically look after the children. Criticisms - Not all policies put women in second place. Equal Pay laws; welfare - benefits for lone parents and equal right to divorce can be seen to challenge patriarchy.

Jacques Donzelot (1997) argues the state uses social policies to regulate people's behaviour by using doctors and social workers to control and change behaviour within families. This process is not equally targeted between classes as poor families are seen as more likely to be a 'problem' in need of 'improvement.' Rachel Condry (2007) study 'Families Shamed', examined the relationship between the state and the family, and its expectations about family responsibilities.

CHANGING FAMILY STRUCTURES (family diversity)

Changing social attitudes have created an increasing diversity of family structures. The number of nuclear families as a proportion of all households has decreased challenging the media's obsession with the cereal packet family (*Edmund Leech*, 1968) as the norm. An increasing number of households are now reconstituted/blended/step-families; same sex families or single-person households highlighting the diversity of family forms in the UK, a point which contradicts the media's continued use of the 'cereal packet family' image in for example advertising.

Characteristics of family diversity identified by *Rapoport and Rapoport* (1982) are:

1. organisational diversity - different patterns of work outside and inside the home, and to changing marital trends resulting in a greater democratisation of domestic labour
2. cultural diversity - from indigenous to migrant households from diverse regions such as Western Europe; Middle Eastern; Southeast Asia etc. bring their own unique family and household composition. Afro-Caribbean households are more likely to be single-parent families while South Asian families are traditionally extended families but increasingly they are favouring more nuclear family households than in the past.
3. social class diversity - is demonstrated through joint conjugal roles in middle-class couples; segregated conjugal roles in working-class families. Middle-classes have a higher proportion of nuclear families compared to inner-city working-classes who have a higher proportion of lone-parent households. In addition extended families are still found in traditional working-class areas of the UK
4. family life course diversity - different stages of family structure during key periods, e.g. newlywed couples; couples having children; retired couples
5. life cycle diversity - which exists between families whose members are from different generations e.g. grandparents having different attitudes to cohabitation and divorce

The above helps explain the reasons for the diversity of family structures away from the traditional nuclear family structure identified by Murdock and Parsons (functionalists).

There are two main ways of explaining the growth in family diversity. As mentioned above, functionalists see the nuclear family as the 'correct' family structure, a point exemplified in Leach's cereal packet family. The New Right are in agreement with functionalists as they too identify the nuclear family as being the 'correct' structure. From this any family diversity away from the nuclear family 'norm' is dysfunctional (the opposite of functional).

In contrast, radical feminism and postmodern perspectives do not see the nuclear family as being the ideal family structure. From these two perspectives any set of relationships can be defined as a family by those people involved.

Giddens identifies these changes to family and marriage as part of the transformation of intimacy. Couples now build their relationships on the quality of their relationships rather than the more traditional obligations of economic dependence or a sense of loyalty. Giddens used the term confluent love to describe what keeps couples together in the modern world.

Changing family structures (diversity) due to the influence of marriage, cohabitation, childbearing, divorce etc.

Marriage Timeline

- 1753 – Clandestine Marriage Act: First time the state regulated marriage
- 1836 – Marriage Act introduces Civil marriages: Marriage becomes a civil institution as well as a religious one
- 1949 – Marriage Act: The main piece of legislation regarding marriage
- 2004 – Civil Partnership Act: The first legally recognized relationship for same-sex couples
- 2013 July: Marriage (Same Sex Couples) Act becomes law, making equal marriage legal
- 2014 by Summer: First same sex weddings to take place

Marriage

- marriage remains popular with most adults being married or re-marrying after divorce
- In 2013 there were 18.2 million families in the UK. Of these, 12.3 million consisted of a married couple with or without children
- since the 1970s the amount of marriages has decreased from 480,000 in 1972 to 283,000 in 2005
- over the past 40 years people tend to get married later (could be due to popularity of cohabitation)
- the number of first marriages has fallen but remarriages have increased especially after the Divorce Reform Act of 1969 and then levelled off

Reasons for decrease in marriage over past 40 years:

- secularization
- people wary of marriage
- acceptance of cohabitation
- women's rights – focus on career and not being a housewife (Sue Sharpe studied working-class girls in 1970 and found concerns were marriage, children etc. In 1990 she found girls' priorities had changed to their career and independence)

Cohabitation – their temporary nature could be contributing towards an increase in lone-parent family structures

Over the past 40 years cohabitation has grown significantly in popularity. The number of opposite sex cohabiting couple families has increased significantly, from 2.2 million in 2003 to 2.9 million in 2013. Eleanor Macklin (1975) identifies four types of motivations for cohabitation:

- temporary casual for convenience
- affectionate dating
- trial marriage
- temporary alternative to marriage
- permanent alternative to marriage

Childbearing – birth rates affect family size e.g. 100 years' ago families had more children, consequently were larger

The growth in cohabitation as helped remove the stigma of births outside marriage to the extent that the number of births outside marriage has increased to around 50% of all births in 2013. At the same time women are having fewer children or having them later in life (2013 average age of becoming a mother increased to 30 years) or indeed remaining childless. Beck (1992) suggests this latter change is due to the increasing contradiction between women's domestic roles and paid employment. But it could also be due to the rising cost of childcare.

Ethnicity also determines the birth rate, and the age that women have children. Overall, Bangladeshi and Pakistani women are the most fertile and the extent of the gap between Indian and Bangladeshi women illustrates the importance of distinguishing between specific ethnic minority groups, rather than treating all Asians as a single category. In most of the ethnic groupings, the birth rate peaked at age 25-29, although for Pakistani women, the peak is at the earlier age of 20-24.

Divorce – an increase in divorce rates could be contributing to more blended and lone-parent families as well as a rise in singlehood in the over 45s

The number of divorces in the UK have risen sharply since the 1970s with around 42% of all marriages ending in divorce. There are several reasons for this increase:

- Legal changes – the 1969 Divorce Reform Act made it easier for women to file for divorce
- Changes in women's position – equal job opportunities meant women were less dependent on their husbands
- Secularisation – declining influence of religion
- Ease – divorce has become easier to obtain
- Stigma – less stigma (socially acceptable) attached to divorce. According to Cockett and Tripp normalisation of divorce has occurred making it easier to deal with a failed marriage
- Higher expectations – couples have higher expectations from their marriage. Allan and Crow found individuals seek fulfilment and divorce if it's not found
- Rise of individualism – Beck (2001) said society today is individualised, and as a result self-expression and independence can put a strain on a marriage

Who divorces?

- age – the younger you get married the more likely to divorce due to money issues; growing apart
- old age – the number of people aged 60+ is increasing due to increased life expectancy; loss of stigma and ever increasing economic freedom for women
- social class – the lower the class position of the breadwinner, the more likely to divorce due to financial problems
- parents – the offspring of divorced parents are more likely to divorce themselves
- region - In 2014 Wales had the highest proportion of divorced adults (9.7%) with Northern Ireland the lowest (5.5%). England (9%) Scotland (8.2%)

However, divorce also adds additional pressures on marriage. But at the same time it's important to recognize marriages do 'end' without couples resorting to formal legal proceedings as they:

1. Separate – separation is where couples effectively end their marriage, but remain legally together and still live under the same roof

2. Empty-shell marriage – where a couple remains legally married but love, sex and companionship are in the past

The effects of the rising divorce rates are open to competing interpretations. For the New Right rising divorce rates are an outcome of permissiveness eroding the family, along with family values. While functionalists are concerned about the decline of the nuclear family caused by increasing family diversity. They see rising divorce rates as evidence of higher expectations between couples resulting in less dysfunctional families. Therefore divorce can be seen to have a positive function.

Marxist feminists' argue rising divorce rates are an outcome of the tensions caused by the dual-burden of capitalism. At home women are forced to undertake unpaid labour, while in the workplace they tend to occupy jobs with low wages. Radical feminists would point out increasing divorce rates are an outcome of the dark-side of family life being more openly discussed allowing women to leave oppressive relationships as well as protecting children from witnessing violent relationships.

Rodgers and Pryor (1998) reviewed 200 studies attempting to find out if divorce had a negative effect on children. Children of separated families have a higher probability of:

- being in poverty and poor housing;
- being poorer when they are adults;
- behavioural problems;
- performing less well in school;
- leaving school/home when young;
- becoming sexually active, pregnant, or a parent at an early age;
- depressive symptoms, high levels of smoking and drinking, and drug use during adolescence and adulthood.

Rodgers and Pryor suggested divorce alone does not cause the above problems but occurred in association with other factors which affected the outcomes when divorce occurred.

Factors affecting outcomes of divorce:

- financial hardship can limit educational achievement;
- family conflict before, during and after separation can contribute to behavioural problems;
- parental ability to recover from distress of separation affects children's ability to adjust
- multiple changes in family structure increase the probability of poor outcomes;
- quality contact with the non-resident parent can improve outcomes.

In contrast Jon Bernardes (1997) studies concluded divorce may be less damaging to children than living with parents in constant conflict.

Whichever argument is seen as the stronger sociologists are interested in the way divorce and remarriage is helping to increase the trend towards family diversity and within this diversity new relationships are emerging. Many families are reconstituted/blended after divorce and as Carol Smart (2001), co-author of 'The Changing Experience of Childhood' found:

- there is no 'hand-book' on how to be a good step-parent as "a new etiquette is still emerging"

Singlehood

The composition of singlehood shows 2.5m people between 45 and 64 living in their own home alone with the number of men living on their own increasing far more than women. So what is driving this growth? American sociologist Eric Kinenberg research identified the following points:

1. more people live alone than ever before because they can afford to and so choose to

2. social media revolution has allowed people to experience the pleasures of social life even when they're living alone

3. growth of individualism

4. young solitaires actively reframe living alone as a mark of distinction and success

Dark-side of the Family

The term 'dark side' refers to abuse within the family, particularly towards women and children. ChildLine, (the confidential helpline for children), statistics indicate the extent to which abuse is conducted by parents. The abuse comes in many forms

- Physical abuse
- Sexual abuse
- Emotional abuse
- Economic deprivation
- Threats of violence

FAMILY DYNAMICS: ROLES AND REALTIONSHIPS WITHIN THE FAMILY

Couples

Elizabeth Bott's (1957) 'Family and Social Network' looks at two contrasting types of conjugal roles: segregated and joint. Segregated conjugal roles involve a clear differentiation between the tasks undertaken by men and women, with each pursuing clearly defined and distinct activities. Joint conjugal roles – where husband and wife share tasks – encourages equal relationships where the differentiation – or 'division of labour' – is much less clear.

- Young and Willmott's (1973) 'The Symmetrical Family' detects a shift in conjugal roles which they see as reflecting a new type of relationship between younger married couples. They detect a growing trend away from traditional segregated roles towards more joint – (symmetrical) forms of relationships. The trend originated with middle class families, but increasingly they envisage, working class families adopting similar arrangements.

- Ann Oakley's (1974) 'The Sociology of Housework' underlines the persisting inequalities in family life. It was the first influential study to consider housework as 'domestic labour' (another form of employment). Her respondents depict their domestic obligations as repetitive, unfulfilling and under-appreciated. She found little to support Young and Willmott's view of family roles being 'symmetrical', with power more equally shared between couples.

- Heidi Hartmann's (1981) found that women who had jobs outside the home remained responsible for the bulk of the housework. Husbands with working wives did not tend to do any more housework than those whose wives did not. Though Hartmann appreciates the growth of working women has given them independence this freedom is often hampered by low-paid work so they are still susceptible to male dominance (patriarchy) both in the home and in wider society.

- The dual-burden coined from Arlie Hochschild's 1989 book, 'The Second Shift' describes the responsibility women have for undertaking their domestic duties on top of their paid employment. Hochschild research studied the "leisure gap" between men and women lives caused by the responsibility for looking after the home and the people living in it.

- Duncombe and Marsden's (1995) research reinforces previous studies revealing inequalities in power and domestic responsibilities. Their female respondents complained that their husbands were indifferent to their role in holding the relationship together and the 'emotional investment' they make. The upshot of this, according to the authors, is that women are frequently saddled with a 'triple shift' of obligations: outside work, housework – and emotional work.

- Delphy and Leonard (1992) recognize men do housework, but it is rather limited. Women make the largest contribution to family life, while men contribute the least but gain the most - women carry out housework and caring roles within the family as well as supporting men in their leisure and work activities. Women also help men emotionally in the home by providing 'trouble free sex' as they argue 'men best unwind post-coitally' while in return men make very little contributions to their spouse's well-being.

Covert and overt power between couples

1. overt power is power you can see such as physical abuse

2. covert power is power which is more difficult for the victim to see as controlling such as the man deciding how much housekeeping his wife should have

- Economic dependency - married women become economically dependent on their husbands especially as once children arrive women give up work in order to look after the children and even when mothers do return to work it is usually part-time rather than full-time employment. This dependency means it is much easier for men to set the agenda over important family decisions.

- Male domination (patriarchal power) - feminists see the family as male dominated as men are the bread-winners and tend to make all the key financial decisions.

- Dobash and Dobash (1995) found that most domestic violence occurs within marriage. They argue, this is due to the institution of marriage giving power to men through their wives dependency on them. Feminists have stressed the significant amount of domestic violence used by men to their own way in the family.

- Edgell (1980) found the important family decisions such as financial issues, tended to be made by the husband, while wives were free to make the trivial decisions on their own such as what 'the evening meal which consists of' or where 'they do the weekly shopping'.

- Jan Phal (1993) research found men tended to control and manage a couple's money.

CHILDREN AND CHILDHOOD

Childhood as an age status is not fixed or universal. The experience and meaning of childhood differs across societies, time periods and between different groups. This means having a childhood is not a natural or inevitable period in a person's life but a socially constructed episode.

This is because historical and cross-cultural studies have shown being a child means different things in different societies. Even in those countries where childhood does exist the period of a person's childhood is age dependent. For example in the UK laws define what a child can or cannot do, for example when a child is compelled to attend to school or is allowed to work.

- childhood experience in pre-industrial society – Aries (1960) 'Centuries of Childhood' argued in the 17th Century childhood did not exist as children were viewed as 'tiny adults' – no real difference between children and adults, from a young age and were viewed as economic assets
- early industrial period and childhood – working-class children worked alongside adults particularly in the factories, mines and mills
- later industrial period and childhood - mid 19th century Factory/Mine Acts (social policies) meant children were no longer able to work, children no longer economic assets and 1870 Education Act – children need to be supported
- 20th century onwards - children are viewed **differently to adults** in need of support and protection, children are put first, helping to create the period known as childhood: toys, clothes, TV programmes, food etc.
- social policy cementing the development of childhood through the age of consent; Factory Acts - Contemporary employment legislation; 1870 Education Act; 1980 Child care Act; 1991 Child Support Act

Neil Postman (1982) states that childhood is disappearing as the 19th century divisions between adults and children are disappearing. Children are able to experience things that previously were only available to adults. Postman argues it is the "Frankenstein Syndrome" effect of the mass media, is largely responsible for this, particularly TV, Internet and social media.

Other sociologists argue there's been an increase in child-centredness in the UK due to families being smaller; increasing affluence along with parents driving their children around more.

However Diana Gittins (1997) argues studies which treat children as one homogenized group fails to recognize the diversity of inequality between childhood experiences such as social class, gender, ethnicity and culture. Hendrick (1997) identified the discourses of childhood as being socially constructed around the Victorian image of the natural and romantic child which possessing a natural innocence. Two later discourses of childhood proposed by Hendrick (1997) were the child as a family member and the child as a state responsibility (child of the welfare state) in need of protection and care.

Note: Now you have finished this unit you might like to test your subject knowledge using our multiple choice test book which is also available to purchase at Amazon.

2 EDUCATION

SCHOOL SYSTEM AND TYPES OF SCHOOLS

In the same way politicians sought to promote certain types of family structures, they have and continue to influence the types of school there are in England and Wales through their social policies.

1944 Education Act – established 3 types of schools known as the tripartite system – grammar; technical and secondary modern schools. A process of selection via 11+ test determined which school you went to. The top 15-20% of those passing the 11+ went to grammar schools

Criticisms of tripartite system:

- 11+ was unreliable;

- the selection process was unfair and wasteful;

- cemented social-class divisions

Comprehensive Schools – unlike the tripartite system there is no selection test for entry to comprehensive schools. The development of comprehensive schools came in the 1960s as a reaction against tripartite system (but process of selection still occurs in some areas of England).

Comprehensives sought to:

- reduce social class divisions;

- break down social-class barriers

Conservative education policy (1979 – 1997)

- New Vocationalism 1986 (NVQs etc);

- The 1988 Education Reform Act introduced competition between schools and turned parents into 'consumers' of education. This process is often termed the marketization (free market) of education. New Right thinkers argue social policies are more effective if they are driven by free market principles. These principles are evident in the 1988 Education Act because the act introduced (in no particular order):

1. The National Curriculum
2. National testing (SATS)
3. National league tables
4. Open enrolment and parental choice
5. Ofsted
6. Local management of schools

New Labour's educational policy 1997 – 2010

- Specialist schools;
- Expansion of league tables (vocational GCSEs added as well as Contextual Value Added Scores);
- Equality of opportunity e.g. EMA; Education Action Zones (known as compensatory education)- page 23
- Expansion of numbers in FE and HE;
- Expansion of vocational education

Conservatives 2010 onwards

- Academies Bill;
- Free Schools:
- Bursary Scheme (replaced EMA);
- Vocational GCSEs axed from league tables;
- Changes to A-levels and GCSES
- Since 2010 there is now an even wider range of schools children can attend: Free schools, traditional Academies and Academy Converters all have the same status in law.

Independent Schools otherwise known as fee-paying schools are independent of government control.

COMPETING PERSPECTIVES OF EDUCATION

Functionalist perspective of education - Emile Durkheim – writing over 100 years ago, argued one of the main functions of education is to bind members of society together – this creates social unity and social solidarity. Therefore like the family, education is seen as a functional prerequisite because it helps pass on society's core values such as the division of labour.

Talcott Parsons writing in the 1950s developed Durkheim's ideas. He identified socialization (secondary) and social integration as two key functions of education, along with role allocation. Like Davis and Moore, Parsons' argued the education system functions to put the right people in the right jobs through a meritocratic system of role allocation.

For functionalists the key functions (purpose) of the education system are:

1. passes on society's culture – education helps establish a value consensus through the hidden curriculum (the hidden curriculum – how students learn behaviours, values, beliefs, and attitudes)
2. socialization - Parsons argues how schools take over the role of parents as sites of secondary socialization.
3. provides a bridge between particularistic values and universalistic values – schooling equips individuals with achieved status rather than ascribed status
4. provides a trained and qualified labour force – schooling equips people in society with the right skills needed to do their jobs creating a division of labour
5. meritocracy - Davis and Moore said the education system becomes the best mechanism for rewarding individual effort legitimising social inequalities

Marxist perspective of education - Louis Althusser (1971) argued that the main role of education in a capitalist society is the reproduction of an efficient and obedient work force. The working-class are 'accept' their exploitation by the ruling-class through several ideological state apparatuses such as the family and the education system. The education system is a particularly powerful ideological state apparatus because:

1. reinforces the ideology that capitalism is just and reasonable (schools teach pupils competition between each other is normal)

2. education system trains future workers to become submissive to authority (schools teaches pupils to accept being told what to do as normal, that way, when your boss orders you what to do, it seems perfectly normal)

Bowles and Gintis' study 'Schooling in Capitalist America' (1976) supported Althusser's ideas that there is a close correspondence (relationship) 'the correspondence principle' between the social relationships in the classroom and those in the workplace through:

1. the correspondence principle – schools processes are very similar to offices and factories, creating a long shadow of work through a system of top-down control and a hidden curriculum encouraging conformity

2. myth of meritocracy - schools legitimate the myth that everyone has an equal chance; so pupils think those people in the top jobs got there on merit when in fact those at the top are there due to their social-class background. In this way social inequality is legitimized and justified as natural
3. hidden curriculum – the school processes mentioned above which prepare students for workplace (rather than scholastic achievement) are reinforced through having to follow a timetable; being punctual; wearing a uniform; doing homework, are all part of the hidden curriculum (the 'visible' curriculum is your lessons, school assemblies, etc).

Bourdieu also sees the education system as reproducing and legitimizing social inequalities through his concept of social capital in order to explain how the middle-classes succeed while the working-class are less likely to (see page 22).

Paul Willis also adopts a Marxist approach when he studied the relationship between the education system and the workplace. His interactionist approach looked at working-class subcultural resistance (counter-culture) to the education system (see page 23).

Both functionalists and Marxists refer to the hidden curriculum. However they have distinct differences:

Functionalism and the hidden curriculum (positive)	Marxism and the hidden curriculum (negative)
1. pupils to look smart via the school uniform	1. school rules, detentions & rewards, teach people to conform whether you like it or not!
2. punctuality through disciplining people who are late	2. school assemblies teach respect for dominant ideas
3. shows children how to follow instructions	3. boys and girls to accept different roles in society with boys learning to be masculine and girls feminine
4. how to read and follow a timetable	4. to follow teachers' instructions without question in the same way you have to follow a bosses orders
5. teaches meritocracy - the benefits of working hard and doing additional work at home (homework)	5. being punctual, as your time belongs to your teacher/school and not you. This again replicates the way a future boss owns your time and so you're being prepared for the world of work!

Both functionalist and Marxist perspectives have other similarities:

- They are both structuralist approaches

- They both tend to ignore social processes within school (factors inside school) – except Willis

- They both tend to ignore the effect of the hidden curriculum on gender stereotyping

Despite their similarities functionalist and Marxist perspectives have their problems:

Problems with functionalism	Problems with Marxism
1. Differences in achievement in terms of gender, ethnicity and class questions the notion of a meritocratic education system 2. Education does not prepare students for the workplace as employers are often critical of the education system 3. It does not adequately explain how education serves the interests of certain groups through promoting certain values and ideologies	1. It assumes pupils are passive victims in the classroom – a point raised by Paul Willis 2. Most people see the inequalities in the education system and some parents challenge it by paying for their child's education 3. Some students work hard to overcome the inherent inequalities in the education system

Feminist perspective of education - for feminists the education system reinforces the social inequalities between the genders. This is achieved through:

1. gendered language – reflecting wider society, school textbooks (and teachers) tend to use gendered language – 'he', 'him', 'his' etc making women invisible
2. gendered roles – school textbooks have tended to present males and females in traditional gender roles – for example, women as mothers and housewives
3. gender stereotypes – reading schemes have also tended to present traditional gender stereotypes e.g 'boys are presented as more adventurous than girls'
4. women in the curriculum – in terms of what's taught in schools – the curriculum – women tend to be missing, in the background, or in second place and so 'hidden' from the curriculum mirroring society
5. subject choice – traditionally certain subjects were often seen as 'boys' subjects' and 'girls' subjects'

Feminist perspectives have been valuable for exposing gender inequality in education. Partly as a result of sociological research, a lot has changed – for example, much of the sexism in reading schemes has now disappeared. Today, women have overtaken men on most measures of educational attainment.

FACTORS INSIDE SCHOOL AND FACTORS OUTSIDE SCHOOL AFFECTING ACHIEVEMENT

Despite numerous forms of social policy interventions by the state, significant class differences in educational achievement continue. Some sociologists focus on factors outside school as the primary cause for social class differences in educational achievement while others focus on factors inside school.

FACTORS OUTSIDE SCHOOL (material, cultural, linguistic deprivation and subcultural explanations)

Material deprivation

- Douglas' (1964) research identified material factors as the cause of working-class underachievement in schools. Material factors include, poor housing, poor diet etc. Gibson and Asthana (1999) found the greater the level of family disadvantage the smaller the percentage of students gaining 5 or more GCSE grades A* - C.

- A more recent piece of research by Lisa Harker (2006) also found a relationship between poor-quality housing and low attainment at school. Harker's research found:

1. less space to play, restricted a child's cognitive development
2. there was less space to study
3. increased likelihood of being bullied at school which increased truancy rates
4. higher stress levels of the parents, leading to less support

- Martha Farah (2006) researched the impact of socio-economic status on cognitive development and found that poverty had a direct impact on the development of a child's brain which ultimately affected their attainment at school.

- Furthermore the Sutton Trust (2005) found a direct relationship between free school meals and attainment. Top performing state schools had around 3% of their intake eligible for free school meals, whereas the majority of state schools had 14.5% of their intake eligible for free school meals.

Cultural deprivation

- Douglas also found cultural factors played an important part in a child's attainment at school. Douglas found middle-class parents compared to working-class parents:

1. took greater the parental interest in a child's education the greater the educational success
2. were better educated themselves and so better understood education system
3. more confident in dealing with schools/teachers
4. better able to help their child with school work

Cultural Capital

Bourdieu uses the term habitus to describe the cultural characteristics and values of each social-class. His point is middle-class children tend to thrive in school, as the culture of schooling is one which engages with cultural capital because:

1. cultural capital – the knowledge, language and values which readily translate into educational capital

2. upper and middle-class children succeed in school as they have more cultural capital

3. working-class children tend to lack cultural capital and so are more likely to fail in an educations system which 'enjoys' cultural capital

4. Bourdieu's point is that school looks like it is culturally neutral when it is biased towards the upper and middle-classes

Subcultural explanations

- Cultural differences are extended further by examining sub-cultural differences between social groups. Sugarman (1970) and Hyman (1967) highlighted the effects of socialization:

    1. Middle-classes socialised their children to – focus on future time orientation and deferred gratification facilitated by individual effort
    2. Working-classes socialised their children to – focus on present time orientation and immediate gratification due to a sense of fatalism

Linguistic deprivation – language and education

- Educational success is heavily dependent on language. Bernstein (1971) distinguished between restricted speech codes (can be used by both social classes but mainly lower working classes) and elaborated speech codes (used by middle-classes).

Compensatory education (positive discrimination) is used by the state to compensate for the social inequalities identified above affecting educational outcomes. Examples are:

    1. Operation Head Start;
    2. Educational Action Zones;
    3. Educational Priority Areas;
    4. Pupil Premium; 16 – 19 Bursary Fund

Factors Inside School (interactionist perspective) school organization, teacher interaction and pupil subcultures

The interactionist perspective does not see pupils as passive 'victims'- of material or cultural forces but as active in their relationships with teachers and their schools e.g. school council influencing the meaning they give to a situation.

School organisation

- Keddie (1971) challenges the notion of cultural deprivation, discussed above, as the root cause of educational failure. Instead Keddie shines the spotlight on schools themselves as failing to meet the needs of cultural diversity.

- Rutter (1979) also places a greater emphasis on schools themselves. The better their organizational structures and polices the better the school; policies such as: (listed overleaf)

1. homework policy
2. marking policy
3. teacher reward systems
4. mixed ability classes
5. teacher lesson preparedness

Teacher interaction

- Becker's research found teachers had a stereotypical image of an ideal pupil based on middle-class qualities, labelling the ideal pupil as bright and successful, the halo-effect. In contrast teachers stereotyped working-class pupils as lacking motivation and difficult to manage therefore are negatively labelled as thick or slow.

- Rosenthal and Jacobson (1968) research found positive and negative labels helped produce a self-fulfilling prophecy in the classroom, highlighting the value of an interactionist approach as pupils clearly 'active' in their relationships with teachers.

- Ball's study of Beachside Comprehensive examined the effect of banding and streaming on pupil performance. Ball found top stream students were warmed up while lower streamed/banded pupils were cooled down. Streaming of banding is often linked to social class – the higher your social class the higher the likelihood of being in a top stream/band.

   1. setting is where pupils of similar ability are put in different groups/sets in specific subjects
   2. streaming/banding involves grouping students of similar ability for every subject studied.

PUPIL SUBCULTURES

Male anti-school subcultures

- Hargreaves (1967) related the emergence of pupil subcultures to labelling and streaming. Colin Lacey's (1970) study of Hightown Grammar school also showed how streaming can lead to the creation of anti-school subcultures. Paul Willis (1997) in 'Learning to Labour' examined the effects of being placed in lower bands/streams. Though Willis adopted a Marxist approach he drew much from the interactionist perspective to compensate for the failings of the traditional Marxist model. Willis found working-class pupils rebelled against their being labelled as failures by acting the fool in lessons in order to enhance their status/self-esteem in ways other than academic ones.

Mac an Ghaill (1994) identified 3 working-class male subcultures

1. Macho Lads;

2. Academic Achievers

3. New Enterprisers

Female subcultures

- Scott Davis (1995) found girls' resistance to school was evident but less aggressive than their male counterparts due to their preoccupation with 'romance' and any future domestic roles. Abrahams (1995) identified female resistance to school as one based on pushing school rules to the limit. While Osler and Vincent (2003) suggest that girls are more likely to develop patterns of non-attendance when facing difficulties in school

- Margret Fuller (1984) found African Caribbean girls formed positive subcultures by working extra hard, determined to succeed despite experiencing racism in schools. In contrast C. Jackson (2006) 'Lads and Ladettes in School: Gender and the Fear of Failure' looked at how girls are forming anti-school subcultures and becoming ladettes because of the fear of academic failure.

African-Caribbean male subcultures

- Gaine and George (1999) found African-Caribbean subcultures develop from both factors inside and outside school.

African-Caribbean female subcultures

- Mac an Ghail (1998) found in general African –Caribbean girls are pro-education and ambitious. Margret Fuller (1984) found African Caribbean girls formed positive subcultures by working extra hard, determined to succeed despite experiencing racism in schools

GENDER DIFFERENCES IN EDUCATIONAL ACHIEVEMENT

Until 1980s the underachievement of girls was the major concern. However since 1990s girls started to outperform boys in all areas of the education system.

At GCSE girls tend to do better in the majority of subjects:

- 63.4% of girls and 53.8% of boys achieved 5+ A*-C GCSEs or equivalent in 2006 – a gender gap of 9.6%
- largest gender differences (a female advantage of more than 10% on those gaining an A*-C GCSE) are for the Humanities, the Arts and Languages
- smaller gender differences (a female advantage of 5% or less) tend to be in Science and Maths subjects
- girls are more likely than boys to gain an A* grade at GCSE
- boys are a little more likely to gain a G grade at GCSE or to gain no GCSEs at all

At A –Level gender differences in pass rate are much narrower but gender differences still remain:

- across all subjects, the range of difference is 4%. This is in the context of a very high pass rate
- girls perform better than boys in terms of those attaining an A grade (for the majority of subjects), which is a significant change over the last ten years

NOTE: Gender is not the strongest predictor of attainment:

- social class attainment gap at Key Stage 4 (as measured by percentage point difference in attainment between those eligible and not eligible for free school meals) is three times as wide as the gender gap
- some minority ethnic groups attain significantly below the national average and their under-achievement is much greater than the gap between boys and girls

Why are girls doing better than boys?

Mitos and Browne (1998) found

1. the women's movement and feminism raised girls' expectations and self-esteem
2. the increasing number of employment opportunities for women
3. many girls' mother are in paid employment and act as positive role models for them
4. girls' priorities have changed: Sue Sharpe (1976) 'Just Like a Girl'
5. girls are better motivated and organised than boys
6. girls at 16 are seen to be more mature than boys
7. girls benefitted from introduction of coursework in GCSEs/A-Levels
8. national curriculum made more subjects compulsory
9. teachers less likely to gender stereotype girls into set roles or careers

Why do boys underachieve?

1. boys are generally more disruptive in class than girls
2. boys appear to gain 'street cred' by not working hard
3. decline in traditional male jobs
4. teachers tend to have lower expectations of boys

5. lack of male role models in schools
6. laddish subcultures
7. identity crisis in men – uncertain future removes purpose in achieving
8. boys do not like reading as it has become feminised
9. boys tend to overestimate their ability
10. feminisation of assessment – coursework rather than competitive exams

Teacher-pupil interaction affecting the gender gap?

1. Michael Barber (1996) found boys tend to over-estimate their ability, with GCSE results showing the opposite to be true
2. Michelle Stanworth (1983) found boys dominated classroom interaction, pushing girls to the margins which lowered their self-confidence and made them feel less valued, hence girls underestimating their ability
3. Dale Spender (1982) found teachers gave priority to boys giving the impression what girls said was less important
4. Howe (1997) identified the different ways teachers interact with boys and girls - such differences in interaction emerge very early, even in preschool.

Masculine identity can be seen as incompatible with academic success

1. **Forde** (2006) boys are more likely to be influenced by their male peer group which might devalue schoolwork and so put them at odds with academic achievement. It is argued that girls do not experience a conflict of loyalties between friends and school to the same extent as boys
2. **Jackson** 2002 found disruptive behaviour will have a number of benefits by increasing a boy's status with his peer group and can it can deflect attention away from academic performance
3. **Kelly** (1987) found science and the science classroom remain 'masculine' environments with boys dominating science classrooms

Are Changes in the Examination System Responsible for the Gender Gap?

1. Stobart (1992) found a direct relationship between the relative improvement of girls' achievement and the weighting and type of coursework required in different subjects
2. Perceptions of girls' perceived advantage in coursework is high amongst teachers. Over half (53%) of teachers felt that that there was a difference between boys' and girls' ability to do coursework Bishop (1996)

Effects of gender socialization

1. **Lobban** (1974) found evidence of gender stereotyping in children's books with women occupying traditional roles. Best (1993) found little had changed in almost 20 years

2. **Kelly** (1987) – gender stereotyping in science classrooms as well as science text books where women are largely invisible

Changes in society

1. Beck (1992) argues in the risk society the rise of individualism allows women to become more self-reliant and self-sufficient through education

Changes in society

ETHNICITY AND ACHIEVEMENT IN SCHOOL

The achievement of ethnic minority pupils in British schools is very complex but the Swann Report of 1985 examined the underachievement of some ethnic minority groups. It is important not to see ethnic minorities as a homogenized (single) group. This is because the patterns of achievement are varied.

Pupils of Indian and Chinese origin tend to do very well, out-performing both the average and the scores of white pupils. By contrast, pupils of Pakistani origin show a very varied pattern of achievement with some doing very well and others relatively poorly. Nevertheless minority ethnic groups tend to underachieve when compared to other population groups.

Your revision will be made easier by using the same approach as used above. Remember to isolate **factors inside school** from those **factors outside school**. Similarly refer back to the previous sections on social-class backgrounds; speech and language codes as well as material and cultural factors.

First some facts (Runnymede Trust, June 2012) which highlight the wide variation across ethnic minority groups:

- Attainment – GCSES (5 A*-C grades including Maths and English) Attainment by ethnicity has improved since 2006/7, and achievement gaps between some ethnic groups and the national level have disappeared. Other ethnic groups, such as Chinese students, have far higher levels of attainment compared to the national level. It is worth highlighting however that Pakistani and Black Caribbean young people still have lower attainment levels than the national level. The data for 2010/11 is as follows:

1. The national level, and the percentage of White British pupils achieving 5 A*-C grades including Maths and English, is 58%. This compares to around 45% in 2006/07

2. Chinese students are the highest attaining group, with 78.5% achieving 5 A*-C grades including Maths and English. This compares to 70% in 2006/07

3. Indian students are the second highest attaining group, with 74.4% achieving 5 A*-C grades including Maths and English. This compares to around 62% in 2006/07

4. Bangladeshi pupils now have a slightly higher attainment rate than White pupils, with 59.7% 5 A*-C grades including Maths and English. This is a massive improvement given that only around 40% achieved this 2006/07, which was 5% less than White pupils and the National Level

5. There has also been an improvement for Black African pupils, with 57.9% achieving 5 A*-C grades including Maths and English, compared to just over 40% achieving this in 2006/07. A similar level of improvement can be seen for mixed White and Black African pupils

6. However, Pakistani and Black Caribbean young people still have lower attainment levels compared to the national level, with 52.6% and 48.6% respectively achieving 5 A*-C grades including Maths and English. This has, however, improved from around 35% for Pakistani and 34% for Black Caribbean pupils in 2006/07

7. Travellers, Gypsies and Roma are still the lowest achieving groups, with 17.5% of Irish Travellers and 10.8% of those from Gypsy or Roma backgrounds achieving 5 A*-C grades including Maths and English.

This has improved from 2006/07 when only 5% of these groups combined achieved the required grades.

Factors Outside School

- Social class and material factors – African-Caribbean and Bangladeshi Asians are more likely to be working-class and in poverty and so have a general material disadvantage while Indian and African Asian children are more likely to come from professional/business middle-class backgrounds and the subsequent advantages

- Language – In some ethnic minority households English is not the main language which might cause problems in doing some school work/communication with teachers – but the Swann Report (1985) found language factors were of little importance for the majority as did Modood (1997) who found the high attainment of Indian pupils suggested a second language was not a barrier to achievement

- Racism outside school – Stuart Hall identified a 'culture of resistance' among African-Caribbean youths as a reaction to racial prejudice in society

- Family life – some minority ethnic groups have stronger parental support than others. African-Caribbean have high levels of lone-parenthood and the subsequent material problems. Tony Sewell (1997) argued African-Caribbean boys growing up in lone parent households lacked male role models found in father figure. In contrast Asian family families tend to be extended families offering high levels of support. In addition Archer (2006) found Chinese students and parents put a high value on education as it gave the family a high standing in their community.

Factors Inside School

- Ethnocentric curriculum - school curriculum and the hidden curriculum is too focused on white British culture and adds to the low self-esteem and underachievement of ethnic minorities.

- Racism inside school - The Swann Report found only a small number of teachers were consciously racist. But - Wright (1992) found teachers treated ethnic minority children differently to White children and Gillborn (1990) found African-Caribbean students were more likely to be criticised compared to other ethnic groups committing the same offence – could this lead to Hargreaves self-fulfilling prophecy or Stuart Hall's culture of resistance? Browne (2008) argues negative labelling does not necessarily lead to the negative effects of the self-fulfilling prophecy – see Fuller page 24.

- Setting and streaming - evidence suggests that Black pupils are more likely to be entered for lower tier exams, meaning that these students are only able to able to achieve a maximum grade of a C grade. Stephen J. Ball (2008) has found that Black Caribbean and African students are less likely to be identified for gifted and talented programmes. In contrast, evidence also suggests that Chinese and Indian students are more likely to be entered into higher sets

- Exclusions and discipline - research by David Gillborn and David Drew (2010) found that excluded pupils are 4 times more likely to finish their education without having gained academic qualification. Research by the former Department for Education and Skills (Getting it, Getting it Right 2006) suggest a number of reasons as to why Black pupils are disproportionately excluded, including institutional racism. The same report also found Black pupils encounter both conscious and unconscious prejudice from teachers (both in terms of frequency and severity).

Note: Now you have finished this unit you might like to test your subject knowledge using our multiple choice test book which is also available to purchase at Amazon.

3 RESEARCH METHODS

Positivism and interpretivism are two distinct principles which shape the reasoning behind research methods:

Positivists use quantitative research methods. These methods produce quantitative data which is information presented in numerical form such as graphs and charts. In contrast sociologists adopting an interpretivist approach to social research prefer to use qualitative research methods. These methods generate qualitative data such as in-depth insights into respondents thoughts and feelings, along with the meanings they give to events rather than numerical data.

The core principles of positivism (quantitative methods) are:

- social scientific research is based on logic with a clear methodology
- research must be objective throughout all processes
- the role of theory is to generate a hypothesis (prediction) which can be tested
- look for cause and effect (patterns of behaviour) in order to uncover universal laws about the social world – what Durkheim termed social-facts
- positivists use quantitative methods

The core principles of interpretivism (qualitative methods) are:

- interpretivists are anti-positivist in principle as they are skeptical about sociology's scientific status
- they reject the view human behaviour is predictable in the same way the natural world is seen to be
- unlike molecules, human beings are conscious entities and act with purpose
- intrepretivists argue human behaviour is not the result of external forces (social facts) instead sociologists need to understand the meaning and motivations behind individual action by seeing the world through their eyes – this is known as verstehen
- interpretivists use qualitative methods

There are two types of quantitative and qualitative data - primary and secondary.

- primary data is that collected by sociologists themselves through social surveys such as structured interviews
- secondary data is data which already exists such as that found in newspapers, novels, literature, letters, diaries, police records, school results, government reports etc.

Positivists prefer to collect quantitative data through the following research methods which are seen to collect reliable data:

- closed/structured questionnaires
- structured interviews
- the experiment
- the comparative method
- official statistics
- social surveys

Interpretivist primary methods include:

- participant and non-participant observations
- open-ended questionnaires
- informal or unstructured interviews

Quantitative secondary sources: a main source of quantitative secondary data comes from official sources such as local and national government and their associated agencies such as the Office for National Statistics (ONS) who gather data on births; deaths; marriages etc. to produce official statistics.

Advantages of official statistics

- they're relatively easy and inexpensive to access
- they're readily available
- they're often the only source of data on a topic area
- as they're so comprehensive they're more likely to be representative
- they're more likely to cover a long time span (crime figures and education data) and so it's easier to see the influence of government policies 'before and after'

Disadvantages of official statistics

- as official data isn't collect by sociologists, problems are likely in the recording and accuracy of the data, for example the British Crime Survey exists to overcome the 'dark-figures' of unrecorded crime
- some of these 'dark figures' come from policemen having to interpret a situation as being criminal or not. This shows how official data might not be as objective as expected
- officials recording data are doing so for administrate reasons and so they're not using terms and classifications used by sociological researchers
- official figures are sometimes 'massaged' by the state to avoid embarrassing the government of the day for example hospital waiting times

Secondary qualitative data is data which already exists such as:

Interpretivist secondary methods include:

- diary entries
- Facebook entries;
- letters and other personal accounts
- newspapers,
- novels
- police records,

- government reports;
- school records;
- /parish registers
- content analysis

Advantages of secondary qualitative data:

- qualitative secondary sources are sometimes the only form of information available on a particular topic. For example Laslett's research on the family across several centuries wouldn't have been possible if records hadn't been kept. This shows how this form of documentation is useful for making comparisons over time
- qualitative secondary sources provide a gateway into the past allowing researchers to understand the concerns and attitudes of people at the time. This can be carried out by reading letter columns in newspapers as well as comment postings on online newspapers such as the Guardian for example
- analysing historical documents is useful in allowing interpretivists to gain insights into the beliefs, values and ideologies held by their authors

Disadvantages of qualitative secondary sources of data:

- how credible is the evidence. An individual diary entry could be full of exaggerations and biases, moreover any entry could merely reflect the interests and beliefs of the author. For example autobiographies and diaries of politicians might contain selected content in order to portray the author in a more positive light
- how representative is the evidence? It could be that other documents which would challenge an account of are ignored in order to keep the author in a positive light, how credible is the evidence? For example newspaper accounts of an incident might reflected the values of the newspaper creating the report

Considerations any sociologist must make when choosing an appropriate method:

- **validity** – to what extent do the research findings provide a true picture of what was studied?
- **reliability** – will the findings be the same if the study is repeated?
- **representativeness** – will the sampling method produce results which are representative of the wider population in order for generalization to be made?
- **ethical issues** – will the research processes be structured around moral standards of behaviour?
- **pilot study** – designing a suitable trial-run in order to achieve a decent response rate
- **practicalities** – is there the time and money to conduct the chosen method?
- **the subjects** – is the selected method appropriate for the chosen respondents?
- **theoretical considerations** – sociologists preferences determines the selected method

Experimental method:

1. Scientists researching the natural sciences (physics, chemistry, biology) conduct their research in laboratories. They start with a hypothesis and use the scientific process to test whether their hypothesis was true or false. In the laboratory all the variables are kept constant expect the independent variable (the one you are testing).
2. In laboratories scientists are able to control the variables (e.g. temperature, light etc.) so an experiment can be undertaken in order to test out a hypothesis (a prediction which can be tested).
3. All the data is converted into numerical form (hence why positivist sociologists seek to do the same

thing).

4. Overcoming the Hawthorne Effect – where the researchers presence affects the behavior of those being studied

There are three types of experiments sociologists can use:

1. Lab experiment
2. Field experiment
3. Natural experiment

The advantages of laboratory experiments are:

- makes isolating and manipulating variables easier so causes of events can be identified
- other scientists can easily repeat the same experiment
- they're high in reliability as other researchers can replicate the same experiment and achieve the same results
- comparisons can be made with similar experimental research
- scientists can test their hypothesis in controlled conditions

The disadvantages of using the experimental method in sociology are:

- it's difficult to identify and isolate a single cause of any social issue such as the cause of crime, as there could be multiple causes
- because of the above, it's impossible to isolate variables for testing on their own in order to see if they are the cause. For example, the causes of underachievement at school could be subcultural or economic or dietary etc.
- as sociologists want to study people in their normal environment any laboratory setting becomes an artificial situation – it's not real life – a point exacerbated by the fact people would know they're being experimented on and so The Hawthorne Effect would undermine the validity of any experiment being conducted
- there are numerous ethical problems for the sociologist, particularly as the experimental group could suffer negative effects from the experiment being conducted on them. Another ethical issue is people might not want to be experimented on in the first place

Field experiments

- Field experiments occur in real-life conditions such as a school, while at the same time trying to follow similar procedures to those found in any laboratory experiment.
- Some experimental methods have been used in sociology and these are known as field experiments. Field experiments are conducted in the real world situations, such as a school. They tend to be carried out by interpretivists who are interested in looking for meanings which underpin everyday interaction in the social world.

Rosenthal and Jacobson conducted a field experiment in a school in 1968. This involved testing the hypothesis teacher expectations hand important effects on pupils academic performance, in order to see if the self-fulfilling prophecy existed.

- the trouble is this form of 'real-world' experiment is fraught with ethical problems as it could have been the teachers expectations and those students labelled with low expectations could have been damaged by the label

- positivists argue field experiments suffer from issues of reliability as the sociologist cannot control all the likely variables

Natural experiments: are conducted in natural environments (a laboratory is an artificial environment). One example would be studies of twins (to test out whether a cause is due to nature or nurture). However though natural experiments are very rare in 2015 NASA astronaut Scott Kelly and his twin, former astronaut Mark Kelly were part of a natural experiment to test the effects of long space missions on humans.

The comparative method

- The comparative method is built on the same principles as the experimental method discussed above but uses the real-world as the laboratory.
- Instead of setting up an experiment the researcher collects data, usually official statistics about different social groups (e.g. working-class; middle-class and upper-class) and then compares one group with another to identify what is evident in one group but not another.

Social surveys

Social surveys are popular with positivist sociologists because they can collect primary data from a large number of people, typically in a standardized statistical form.

1. The sociologist takes a random selection of a sample, which is representative of the population being studied.
2. This sample might be sent a standardized questionnaire through the post or asked to take part in a structured interview.
3. The benefit of this method is a large amount of data is compiled in a short time frame.

Some important social survey terms:

- Survey population – is the whole group being studied
- Sampling frame – is a list of names of all those included in the survey population from which the sample is selected
- Representative sample – a small group drawn from the survey population
- Sampling method – the techniques used to select a representative sample
- Hypotheses – is a statement which makes a prediction which is tested to either be true or false by the research
- Operationalisation – is a way of measuring an abstract concepts such as social-class

Most social surveys are conducted via postal questionnaires because:

Advantages of postal questionnaires:

- Tend to be cheap
- Can use larger samples
- Have a quick turnaround period
- Can be closed questions which are user-friendly
- Easily quantified

Disadvantages of postal questionnaires:

- Can be costly in regard to stamp prices
- Need return envelops
- Respondent needs incentive to return questionnaire
- Low response rate
- May not be representative
- Cannot control who completed questionnaire

Before you can give out a survey you need a sample:

Sampling: provides the researcher with a representative sample. A **sampling method** is chosen in order to achieve the most representative sample possible.

The main sampling methods are:

- **Random sampling** – people selected at random
- **Stratified random sampling** – a random sample is chosen from a subdivided group of people e.g. a specific age range
- **Quota sampling** – researcher selects people by a certain criteria e.g. gender
- **Snowball sampling** – the researcher selects a respondent meeting their requirements, then asks them to recommend someone meeting the same criteria
- **Cluster or multistage sampling** – selecting your sample in various stages e.g. 1st – take a random sample of hospital patients; 2nd – select a random sample from within those patients for your study
- **Systematic sampling** – selecting from the sampling frame at regular intervals until the size of sample is reached

Pilot study - once the researcher has selected their research method and their sample method it is a good idea to conduct a pilot study. A pilot study is a practice run, so you iron-out any logistical problems or issues with the questions being asked.

Questionnaires

- Questionnaires (like the postal questionnaire discussed above) are a common method of discovering sociological truths. If you're using positivist methods you'll have to make a closed or structured or pre-coded questionnaire in order to gather quantitative data.
- On the other hand, as a sociologist, you might wish to adopt an interpretivist approach and use open-ended or unstructured questionnaires.

Closed or structured or pre-coded questionnaires (quantitative)

Advantages

1. relatively quick to complete by respondent
2. easier, quick, and less costly to analyze
3. data produced ought to be reliable, (easy to repeat) allowing other researchers to test the findings (replicating the method of the natural scientists)
4. they produce data which is relatively easy to categorize and present in statistical form such as graphs and charts

5. make it easy for comparisons to be between different groups. This is because respondents are all answering the same questions

Disadvantages

1. possible misinterpretation of questions
2. limited choice of answers puts artificial limits on how the respondent answers
3. if answered with researcher present respondent might 'lie', as they're too embarrassed to tell the truth
4. the responses set out are those of the sociologist and not necessarily those of the respondent (imposition problem)
5. too many options might confuse the respondent
6. no way of knowing if respondent understood the question/questions
7. response options can put ideas into the respondents mind

Open or unstructured questionnaires (qualitative)

Advantages

1. responses are in the respondents own words, rather than those of sociologist as with closed questionnaires, which improves validity
2. the imposition problem found in closed questionnaires is less of an issue as the respondent is using their own words and not those of the researcher, as with closed questionnaires
3. they provide more detailed and deeper answers, including more information such as feelings and attitudes
4. open-ended questions simply do not allow respondents to speed read or avoid reading the questions and so "fill in" the answer without thinking

Disadvantages

1. with such a broad range of answers it can be hard to classify and quantify the data into graphs and charts
2. with such a broad range of answers it can be difficult to compare results with similar research
3. response rate can be lower than with those that use closed-ended questions, as people have to fill them in and they might feel awkward regarding their spelling and or hand-writing
4. responses might be 'skip' to the point as the respondent is in a rush and so the answers given are too vague
5. hand-writing might be illegible through the respondent rushing

Interviews

Structured Interviews (quantitative)

Advantages

1. There is less of a problem with interviewer bias than unstructured (open interviews) as there's less involvement of the interviewer
2. As they usually have pre-planned (pre-coded) questions, it's relatively easy to put the data gathered into statistical forms such as graphs (positivist in nature)
3. As the questions are pre-coded the data gathered is often seen as more reliable as all respondents are answering the same questions, which makes it easier to replicate the process by other interviewers

4. They're generally seen as a more effective way of getting questionnaires completed, particularly postal questionnaires which have a high non-response rate, particularly as it overcomes the problems of illiteracy

Disadvantages

1. Their pre-coded structure means it puts limits on what respondents can say a) which means the interviewer can't probe the respondent beyond what the set questions, b) these limitations mean it's difficult for the interviewer to gain understanding (verstehen) of what the respondents means
2. Although the advantage is seen to be the lack of interviewer bias, there is still remains a possibility of interviewer bias caused by non-verbal cues such as frowning
3. In regard to postal questionnaires and questionnaires, interviews are more costly (interviewers have to be paid and the interview process is much slower) than either postal questionnaires or questionnaires

Unstructured Interviews (qualitative)

Advantages

1. Often a good deal of rapport develops between interviewer and interviewee allowing detailed and honest information to be obtained. This is very useful where the subject being researched might be particularly sensitive
2. It allows the respondent (interviewee) to speak for themselves, so the researcher can gain a better understanding (verstehen) of the topic being discussed
3. The interviewer can easily develop points raised by the respondent to gain an even deeper meaning by exploring the meanings and motivations behind a particular action or event

Disadvantages

1. The success of the interview often depends on the quality and skills of the interviewer
2. The interview itself can be very time consuming and playing back what's been recorded is also very time consuming which means fewer interviews take place meaning samples tend to be small
3. As the interviews are open, the lack of non-standardized questions make generalization and the production of statistics difficult
4. There's a good chance of interviewer bias: a) The interviewer could give non-verbal cues such as smiling which could influence an interviewee's response b) The interviewer may only follow up leads in the interview they deem important, which could contradict what the respondent feels as important
5. The fact you ask questions about something sometimes affects the dynamic of the interview to the extent the respondent changes their behaviour

Observations

When conducting participant observation the researcher can either observe covertly or overtly.

- Overt observation is where the researcher will disclose themselves to the participants so they know they're being observed.
- Covert observation is where those being observed are unaware they are being observed (the researcher's undercover – 'gone native'); this usually involves the researcher assuming a false identity for example, if you were researching the behaviour of football supporters you'd pretend you were a supporter so you could conduct the research.

A famous example was John Howard Griffin who dyed his skin black and lived as a black man in the southern states of America in 1960.

Advantages of participant observation

1. you have high validity doesn't disturb the normal behaviour of the group – no risk of the Hawthorne effect
2. no prior knowledge of social dynamic being observed is required
3. allows the observer to dig deeper into groups/individual behaviour
4. research can be sustained over a long period of time giving greater depth
5. seen as being high in validity -can see how people really behave
6. it can generate new ideas and insights not previously considered
7. observes first-hand in non-artificial surroundings
8. as they are over a sustained period, you can observe changes in behaviour over-time rather than as snapshot picture
9. only way to observe criminal gangs or other hostile groups
10. Hawthorne Effect

Disadvantages of participant observation

1. ethical issues just by participating in criminal activity
2. ethical issues if covertly witnessing criminal activity
3. tend to be small scale and the group being studied might not be typical
4. the researcher may be exposed to danger for example, if participating in criminal activity
5. if the identity of researcher is uncovered the whole research could be ruined
6. the participants may feel betrayed and used if/when they find out their activities were being recorded and could take out revenge
7. difficult to record observations without being found out
8. difficult to leave the group having been a part of the group for so long
9. difficult to remain covert for long periods of time

Positivists question the reliability of participant observation because they are difficult to replicate and so check the validity of any findings. Non- participant observation is conducted when the sociologists observes people in their normal setting without the presence of the researcher to avoid Hawthorne Effect for example observing a teacher via video camera.

Ethnographic studies

- Are sometimes better known as anthropological studies, where the researcher observes a culture by joining the group
- They are small-scale fieldwork producing qualitative data that are seen as valid as the research is conducted in natural settings
- It's hard to make any generalizations from these studies as they're small-scale

Secondary sources of data

Secondary sources of data can be quantitative and qualitative

Quantitative secondary sources: a main source of quantitative secondary data comes from official sources such as local and national government and their associated agencies such as the Office for National Statistics (ONS) who gather data on births; deaths; marriages etc. to produce official statistics (see page 33)

Content analysis

Content analysis involves the analysis of 'messages' in mass media content such as TV programmes, newspapers, magazines etc. (secondary sources) which can generate both quantitative and qualitative data.

Strengths

- Low cost
- Can make comparisons over time (longitudinal study)
- Quantitative analysis is seen as reliable

Weaknesses

- Time consuming
- Qualitative studies are highly subjective
- Assumes the media has had an effect on the audience
- Personal documents

Secondary qualitative data is data which already exists such as:

Diaries; letters; etc which provide a rich source of qualitative data on feeling; motives etc (see page 33)

Strengths

- Provide a rich insight into a person's feelings and motivations
- They are usual in providing insights where no other data exists such as being held captive
- They are often the only insight sociologists have into the past such as war veterans diaries or letters home
- Personal documents can supplement official data such as school performance. A school might be high in league tables but pupils dislike the regime in which they learn

Weakness

- They are a one person view of events which can be biased in order to justify a person's actions and therefore invalid
- The data is likely to be unreliable
- The data is likely to be unrepresentative

- The authenticity of the data is open to question
- The sociologist might interpret the data in a way the author never intended

Case Studies and life histories

- Case studies are where the sociologist undertakes an intensive study of the topic or case being studied usually using interpretivist methods such as open-interviews or participant observations.

- Life histories study one individual again through interpretivist methods such as unstructured interviews along with any personal documents to validate what is said.

Strengths of case studies and life histories

1. useful in generating new hypotheses
2. allows the researcher to see the world from another perspective

Weakness

1. may not be representative
2. any interpretation of past events is seen from a contemporary perspective

Historical and public documents

- These are reports made by governments; companies; trade unions; schools; hospital trusts etc; therefore they can be contemporary (current) or historical (from the past).

Strengths of public and historical documents are:

- They are more than likely the only way we can gain insights into past events
- They allow comparisons over time for example, birth; death and marriage rates
- They are useful when assessing the outcomes of various social policies such as raising the school leaving age

Weaknesses of public and historical documents

- The validity of the documents are open to question, as they may have been written selectively
- The documents content is open to misinterpretation
- The authenticity of a document is open to question as it might not have been written by the person it is attributed to; therefore undermining its reliability

Triangulation sometimes referred to as methodological pluralism

- Triangulation is the use of one or more research methods when carrying out social research in order for the different methods to complement each other.

- For example, Ofsted using overt observations as well as official data (exam results) to assess how well as school is performing. The trouble is triangulation produces a lot of data which takes a long time to process.

Longitudinal studies

Data is collected at regular intervals over a period of years.

Strengths

- provide detailed analysis of changes over time e.g. Seven-UP TV programme
- as with Seven-UP the sample remained the same, providing possible evidence of causes to any recorded changes
- as with Seven-UP recorded data is high in validity as not dependent on human memory for data which is liable to forgetfulness or exaggeration

Weaknesses

- as with Seven-UP sample size might dwindle due to people withdrawing or dying
- the Hawthorne Effect
- continuing such studies over time can be costly

Note: Now you have finished this unit you might like to test your subject knowledge using our multiple choice test book which is also available to purchase at Amazon.

4 GLOSSARY

Anthropology – studying the societies and cultures, especially those of pre-industrial societies found around the globe

Bourgeoisie – a term from Marxism denoting a social-class composed of people whose livelihood comes from the ownership of capital

Capitalism – an economy based on the production of goods for sale (commodities) using waged labour; capitalists own the means of production in order to make profit.

Culture – the beliefs, values and customs of a society or social group

Ethnicity – the members of a social group who share common characteristics such as religion, language or race

Ethnography – a research method based on the detailed observation of a culture or group

Experiment/laboratory experiment –a research procedure which attempts to test a hypothesis by manipulating aspects of reality to see whether the outcome suggested by the hypothesis occurs.

Ideology – a system of ideas and beliefs which may reflect the interests of a particular social group

Institutional racism – discrimination against a particular ethnic or racial groups which is built on the processes, procedures and policies of an institution whether or not the discrimination is intended

Marketization of education - where parents have the power and choice to make a decision and "shop around" as consumers of education to see which is the best school to send their child to

Net-migration - The rate of people moving into a country less the number of people moving out of the same country

Patriarchy – a social system of male dominance based on assumptions of male superiority

Power – the capacity of individuals, groups, or social-classes to achieve goals and protect interests

Proletariat – a term from Marxism denoting a social-class of people whose livelihood comes from selling their labour in exchange for wages (see bourgeoisie)

Racism – belief that biologically rooted characteristics determine social activities and abilities as well as the inherent superiority and inferiority of different races

Self-fulfilling prophecy – happens when people act in response to behaviour which has been predicted of them which subsequently makes the prediction come true

Social class – classifications of people with broadly similar occupations, resources or styles of living

Social policy - are public services that aid the well-being of citizens

Society – the total entity formed by individuals and groups and their social relations most commonly located within a nation state

Stereotyping – where generalized qualities or attributes of a social group often prejudice the representation of that group

State – a set of institutions and system of government which exercises control over a specific geographical area and the population of that area.

Underclass – a concept used to characterize those occupying the lowest positions in society

Vocational education - educational training that provides practical experience in a particular occupational field such as learning a trade

Welfare state – the social and political institutions by which the state assumes a responsibility for the health and social welfare of its citizens

5 INDEX

Sociology Revision
AS-Level
Test Yourself

SOCIOLOGYTWYNHAM.COM

ACKNOWLEDGEMENT

Special thanks to pixabay.com for allowing the use of their image on the front cover.

CONTENTS TEST YOURSELF SECTION

PLEASE NOTE

This test yourself booklet has been designed so you can assess the extent of your subject knowledge in the multiple-choice questions section and evaluate your understanding in the short questions section.
Our AS-Level revision guide has been designed to accompany this booklet so you can learn from any misunderstandings in order to improve your learning and examination performance.

1 FAMILY - MULTIPLECHOICE QUESTIONS

Q1 - Parsons said the family has two basic functions. These two functions are:

A – the primary socialization of children and the stabilization of children's personalities

B – the stabilization of adult personalities along with the secondary socialization of children

C – the secondary socialization of children and stabilization of children's personalities

D – the primary socialization of children and the stabilization of adult personalities

Q2 – As radical feminists Delphy and Leonard argue it is:

A – women rather than capitalism who benefit the most from exploiting men and the family is central in maintaining this structure

B – men rather than capitalism who benefit the most from exploiting women and the family is central in maintaining this structure

C – men rather than Marxism who benefit the most from exploiting women and the family is central in maintaining this structure

D - men rather than functionalism who benefit the most from exploiting women and the family is central in maintaining this structure

Q3 – In addition, coming from a radical feminist perspective Delphy and Leonard also argue:

A – families are structured; in this structure women dominate while men and children are subordinate (very few families are patriarchal)

B – families are structured; in this structure men dominate while women and children are subordinate (very few families are matriarchal)

C – most families are matriarchal; in this structure women dominate while men and children are subordinate (very few families are patriarchal)

D – families are structured; in this structure men and women are subordinate to children due to the 1989 Children's Act

Q4 - Marxist feminists argue women's oppression benefits capitalism. Benston argues:

A – feminism benefits from a large army of women – an unpaid workforce - who are compliant and willing to do as they're told because women have been socialized to act this way by other women subsequently women rear future workers to think the same way.

B – via the 1989 Children Act, children benefit from a large army of women – an unpaid workforce - who are compliant and willing to do as they're told because women have been socialized to act this way

C – new right thinkers like Charles Murray benefit from a large army of women – an unpaid workforce – who are compliant and willing to do as they're told and form an underclass

D - capitalism benefits from a large army of women – an unpaid workforce - who are compliant and willing to do as they're told because women have been socialized to act this way and women rears future workers to think the same way

Q5 - Marxist and radical feminist both argue the following:

A – Marxist feminists argue the abolition of the family is needed to end women's oppression but radical feminists disagree

B – Both radical and Marxist feminists argue the family is a functional prerequisite and is needed to end women's oppression

C – Both radical and Marxist feminists argue the abolition of the family is needed to end women's oppression

D - Radical feminists argue the abolition of the family is needed to end women's oppression but Marxist feminists disagree

Q6 – New Right perspectives of the family are very similar to those of:

A – Marxist feminists

B – functionalists

C – Marxist

D – Radical feminists

Q7 – "The breadwinner husband and homemaker-wife model is the best structure for self-reliance, reducing the likelihood of welfare dependency" is a statement best attributed to:

A – Benston a Marxist feminist

B - Delphy and Leonard both with radical feminist perspectives

C - John Redwood a Conservative MP with a New Right perspective

D – Zaretsky from a Marxist perspective

Q8 – When discussing pre-industrial families sociologists are referring to a time period:

A – after the industrial revolution

B – during the industrial revolution

C – during the industrial revolution, but on a Friday afternoon

D – before the industrial revolution

Q9 - During the industrialization period the function (purpose) of the family was multifunctional. These functions were:

A - economic production; educational; political and ascribed status

B - economic production; educational and political

C - economic production; educational; political; ascribed status and discipline

D – educational and political

Q10 - Parsons argues the nuclear family best meets the needs of industrial society as it allows individuals to:

A – work hard

B – form a family

C – eat well

D – achieve their status

Q11 – The stabilization of adult personalities occurs via:

A – hard work

B- sexual division of labour

C – economic production

D – ascribed status

Q12 – The instrumental and expressive roles adopted by adults in a nuclear family are known collectively by functionalists as:

A – the dual burden

B – the triple shift

C – matriarchy

D - the sexual division of labour

Q13 – The importance of primary socialization for Parsons is its establishment of:

A – a value consensus

B- the myth of meritocracy

C – the consumption of goods to aid capitalism

D – patriarchal power

Q14 – For Parsons the benefit of the isolated nuclear family is its capacity:

A – in being free from binding obligations to wider kin as well as being geographically and socially mobile

B - in being geographically and socially mobile

C - in being free from binding obligations to wider kin

D – to impose the sexual division of labour without any intrusion from nosey relatives

Q15 – Although Parsons argues the isolated nuclear family was an outcome of industrialization, other sociologists like Laslett disagree because:

A - Laslett argues nuclear families were the norm in pre-industrial England

B – Laslett argues symmetrical families were the norm during industrialization

C - Laslett argues lone parent families were the norm during industrialization

D – Laslett argues same sex families were the norm during pre-industrial England

Q16 - Social policy refers to:

A – government legislation and activities which seek to undermine the wellbeing of its people

B – government legislation and activities which seek to improve the wellbeing of elderly people

C – government legislation and activities which seek to improve the wellbeing of its people

D - to government legislation and activities which seek to improve the wellbeing of just children

Q17 - In 1945 The Welfare State was a social policy set up to allow the state to support families through:

A – welfare benefits and education

B – welfare benefits, housing, the-right-to-vote, health-care and education

C – housing, the-right-to-vote, education and health-care

D – welfare benefits, housing, health-care and education

Q18 - From 1979 the Conservative Government wanted to protect traditional family by introducing a social policy which 'kept tabs on errant fathers'. The agency which was established in 1993 to collect child maintenance payments is known as:

A – Child Welfare Agency (CWA)

B – Children's Income Agency (CIA)

C – Child Support Agency (CSA)

D – Children's Cash Agency (CCA)

Q19 – Feminists' argue all governmental social policies are prejudicial against women because:

A – Conservatives and the New Right social policies seek to keep women in the home while New Labour might recognize family diversity but their social policies see women as being matriarchal

B - Conservatives and the New Right social policies seek to keep women in the home while New Labour might recognize family diversity but their social policies see women as being the primary carer

C – Conservatives and the New Right social policies seek to keep women out of the home while New Labour might recognize family diversity but their social policies see women as being the primary carer

D - Conservatives and the New Right social policies seek to keep men in the home while New Labour might recognize family diversity but their social policies see men as being the primary carer

Q20 - New Right thinkers argue social policies should be designed to support the nuclear family. Feminists are critical of this way of thinking because:

A – the New Right assume the matriarchal nuclear family is 'natural' rather than socially constructed

B – the New Right assume the patriarchal nuclear family is socially constructed

C – the New Right assume matriarchal nuclear family is socially constructed

D – the New Right assume the patriarchal nuclear family is 'natural' rather than socially constructed

Q21 – Giddens argues couples now build their relationships on the quality of their relationships rather than the more traditional obligations of economic dependence or a sense of loyalty. This is known as:

A – confluent love

B – convergent love

C – consistent love

D – conflicted love

Q22 - The characteristics of family diversity identified by *Rapoport and Rapoport* (1982) are:

A – organizational diversity, social-class diversity, family life course diversity and life cycle diversity

B – cultural diversity, social-class diversity, family life course diversity and life cycle diversity

C – cultural diversity, organizational diversity, social-class diversity, family life course diversity and life cycle diversity

D - cultural diversity, health diversity, organizational diversity, social-class diversity, family life course diversity and life cycle diversity

Q23 Gay and lesbian households, single-person households, lone-parent families, dual-worker families and reconstituted families are all examples of:

A – cereal packet families

B- family homogeneity

C – family diversity

D – the dark-side of family life

Q24 – The term cereal packet family is an image giving the impression that most people live in a 'typical family' which:

A – the husband is the 'breadwinner', with a wife who stays at home in order to look after the children and do the housework. Both these parents are married to each other and neither has been married before.

B - the husband is the 'breadwinner', with a wife who stays at home in order to look after the children and do the housework. Both these parents are married to each other but one of them might have been married before.

C - the husband is the 'breadwinner', with a wife who stays at home in order to look after the children and do the housework. Both these parents are married to each other but one of them has been married before bringing their children from the previous relationship with them

D - the husband is the 'breadwinner', with a male 'wife' who stays at home in order to look after the children and do the housework. Both these parents are a same-sex married couple and neither has been married before.

Q25 - Over the past 40 years cohabitation has grown in popularity. Eleanor Macklin identifies 5 motivations for this increase in popularity:

A – affectionate dating, trial marriage, temporary alternative to marriage and permanent alternative to marriage

B – secularization, people wary of marriage, acceptance of cohabitation and women's rights

C – secularization, people wary of marriage, acceptance of cohabitation, gay rights and women's rights

D - temporary casual - for convenience, affectionate dating, trial marriage, temporary alternative to marriage and permanent alternative to marriage

Q26 - Sue Sharpe studied working-class girls in 1970 and found the girls' concerns were marriage, children etc. In 1990 she found girls' priorities had changed to their career and independence. Her findings could help explain the decline decrease in marriage over past 40 years because:

A – it highlighted the growth in secularization

B – it highlighted the acceptance of cohabitation

C – it highlighted the increasing influence of women's rights – focus on career and not being a housewife

D – it highlighted the increasing influence of gay rights

Q27 - The number of births outside marriage has increased to around 50% of all births in 2013. One explanation for this decrease could be due to:

A – The decrease in cohabitation as helped remove the stigma of births inside marriage

B – The growth in cohabitation as helped remove the stigma of births outside marriage

C – The growth in cohabitation as helped increase the stigma of births outside marriage

D - The decrease in cohabitation as helped remove the stigma of births outside marriage

Q28 - Women are having fewer children or having them later in life (in 2013 the average age of becoming a mother increased to 30 years) or indeed remaining childless. One explanation for this increase could be due to:

A – Beck suggests this latter change is due to the decreasing contradiction between women's domestic roles and paid employment

B – Beck suggests this latter change is due to women conducting less domestic roles and more paid employment

C – Beck suggests this latter change is due to women conducting more domestic roles and less paid employment

D - Beck suggests this latter change is due to the increasing contradiction between women's domestic roles and paid employment

Q29 - The number of divorces in the UK have risen sharply since the 1970s with around 42% of all marriages ending in divorce. One explanation for this could be higher expectations of marriage. Allan and Crow explains this as meaning:

A - individuals seek fulfilment from marriage and divorce if it's not found

B - individuals seek nothing particular from marriage and divorce as something to do

C - individuals seek fulfilment from marriage and divorce when fulfilled

D – individuals seek fulfilment from marriage and so divorce so they can remarry

Q30 - The number of divorces in the UK have risen sharply since the 1970s with around 42% of all marriages ending in divorce. One explanation is secularization; secularization is:

A - declining influence of religion on society

B – increasing influence of religion on society

C – static influence of religion on society

D – confirmation of religion never having had any influence on society

Q31 – An empty shell marriage is:

A – where a couple divorces but decide to cohabit

B- where a couple remains legally married but only sexual relations remain

C - where a couple remains legally married but love, sex and companionship are in the past

D - where a couple divorce but love, sex and companionship remain

Q32 - Marxist feminists' argue rising divorce rates are an outcome of the tensions caused by the dual-burden of capitalism. The dual-burden is:

A – where women are forced to undertake unpaid labour at home, while in the workplace they tend to occupy jobs with no wages

B – where women are forced to undertake unpaid labour at home, while in the workplace they tend to occupy jobs with low wages

C – where women are forced to undertake well-paid labour at home, while in the workplace they tend to occupy jobs with low wages

D - where women are forced to undertake unpaid labour at home, while in the workplace they tend to occupy jobs with high wages

Q33 - Radical feminists would point out increasing divorce rates are an outcome of the dark-side of family life being more openly discussed allowing women to:

A – remain in oppressive relationships while protecting children from witnessing violent relationships

B – remain in oppressive relationships but are free to choose whether to work or not

C – leave oppressive relationships as well as protecting children from witnessing violent relationships

D – leave oppressive relationships but return to them when the situation has calmed down

Q34 - The term 'dark side' of the family refers to:

A – a family home having its electricity supply cut-off due to welfare cuts

B – every family member being unemployed and on welfare

C - abuse within the family, particularly towards women and children

D – the continuing increase in divorce rates

Q35 - Elizabeth Bott's 'Family and Social Network' looks at two contrasting types of conjugal roles: segregated and joint. Segregated and joint conjugal roles are:

A – Segregated conjugal roles where husband and wife share tasks. Joint conjugal roles with little or no differentiation between the tasks

B – Segregated conjugal roles involves no clear differentiation between a husband and wife's tasks. Joint conjugal roles with huge differentiation between the tasks

C – Segregated conjugal roles involve a clear differentiation between the tasks undertaken by men and women. Joint conjugal roles where husband and wife share tasks with little or no differentiation between the tasks

D – Segregated and joint conjugal roles is another term used to describe Elizabeth Bott's concept of the sexual division of labour

Q36 - Wilmott and Young's 'The Symmetrical Family' detects a shift in conjugal roles moving away from traditional segregated roles towards more:

A – asymmetrical forms of relationships

B – same sex relationships

C – segregated forms of relationships

D - symmetrical forms of relationships

Q37 - Duncombe and Marsden's research reinforces previous studies revealing inequalities in power and domestic responsibilities. They coined the term the 'triple-shift' to describe the burden placed on women. The term 'triple-shift' refers to:

A – voluntary work, paid work outside the home, housework and emotional work

B – voluntary work, housework and emotional work

C – housework, trouble-free sex and paid work outside the home

D – paid work outside the home, housework and emotional work

Q38 - Married women become economically dependent on their husbands especially as once children arrive women give up work in order to look after the children. Phal's research found the consequence of this on a woman's economic position within a marriage is:

A – the married couple's roles became more symmetrical

B – men tended to control and manage a couple's money

C – women tended to control and manage a couple's money as they were at home all day

D – children tended to be included more in any financial decision making

Q39 - Neil Postman argues childhood is disappearing as children are able to experience things that previously were only available to adults. What term does Postman use to describe the influence of the mass media on the erosion of childhood?

A – Dracula Syndrome

B – Horror Syndrome

C - Frankenstein Syndrome

D – Childhood Syndrome

Q40 – What do you understand by the term child-centeredness:

A – where children put parents first

B – where siblings put each other first

C – where parents put their children first

D – where children put themselves first

2 FAMILY - MULTIPLE CHOICE QUESTIONS: THE ANSWERS

Q1 - Parsons said the family has two basic functions. These two functions are:

D – the primary socialization of children and the stabilization of adult personalities

Q2 – As radical feminists Delphy and Leonard argue it is:

B – men rather than capitalism who benefit the most from exploiting women and the family is central in maintaining this structure

Q3 – In addition, coming from a radical feminist perspective Delphy and Leonard also argue:

B – families are structured; in this structure men dominate while women and children are subordinate (very few families are matriarchal)

Q4 - Marxist feminists argue women's oppression benefits capitalism. Benston argues:

D - capitalism benefits from a large army of women – an unpaid workforce - who are compliant and willing to do as they're told because women have been socialized to act this way and women rears future workers to think the same way

Q5 - Marxist and radical feminist both argue the following:

C – Both radical and Marxist feminists argue the abolition of the family is needed to end women's oppression

Q6 – New Right perspectives of the family are very similar to those of:

B – functionalists

Q7 – "The breadwinner husband and homemaker-wife model is the best structure for self-reliance, reducing the likelihood of welfare dependency" is a statement best attributed to:

C - John Redwood a Conservative MP with a New Right perspective

Q8 – When discussing pre-industrial families sociologists are referring to a time period:

D – before the industrial revolution

Q9 - During the industrialization period the function (purpose) of the family was multifunctional. These functions were:

A - economic production; educational; political and ascribed status

Q10 - Parsons argues the nuclear family best meets the needs of industrial society as it allows individuals to:

D – achieve their status

Q11 – The stabilization of adult personalities occurs via:

B- sexual division of labour

Q12 – The instrumental and expressive roles adopted by adults in a nuclear family are known collectively by functionalists as:

D - the sexual division of labour

Q13 – The importance of primary socialization for Parsons is its establishment of:

A – a value consensus

Q14 – For Parsons the benefit of the isolated nuclear family is its capacity:

A – in being free from binding obligations to wider kin as well as being geographically and socially mobile

Q15 – Although Parsons argues the isolated nuclear family was an outcome of industrialization, other sociologists like Laslett disagree because:

A - Laslett argues nuclear families were the norm in pre-industrial England

Q16 - Social policy refers to:

C – government legislation and activities which seek to improve the wellbeing of its people

Q17 - In 1945 The Welfare State was a social policy set up to allow the state to support families through:

D – welfare benefits, housing, health-care and education

Q18 - From 1979 the Conservative Government wanted to protect traditional family by introducing a social policy which 'kept tabs on errant fathers'. The agency which was established in 1993 to collect child maintenance payments is known as:

C – Child Support Agency (CSA)

Q19 - Feminists argue all governmental social policies are prejudicial against women because:

B - Conservatives and the New Right social policies seek to keep women in the home while New Labour might recognize family diversity but their social policies see women as being the primary carer

Q20 - New Right thinkers argue social policies should be designed to support the nuclear family. Feminists are critical of this way of thinking because:

D – the New Right assume the patriarchal nuclear family is 'natural' rather than socially constructed

Q21 – Giddens argues couples now build their relationships on the quality of their relationships rather than the more traditional obligations of economic dependence or a sense of loyalty. This is known as:

A – confluent love

Q22 - The characteristics of family diversity identified by *Rapoport and Rapoport* (1982) are:

C – cultural diversity, organizational diversity, social-class diversity, family life course diversity and life cycle diversity

Q23 Gay and lesbian households, single-person households, lone-parent families, dual-worker families and reconstituted families are all examples of:

C – family diversity

Q24 – The term cereal packet family is an image giving the impression that most people live in a 'typical family' which:

A – the husband is the 'breadwinner', with a wife who stays at home in order to look after the children and do the housework. Both these parents are married to each other and neither has been married before.

Q25 - Over the past 40 years cohabitation has grown in popularity. Eleanor Macklin identifies 5 motivations for its increase in popularity:

D - temporary casual - for convenience, affectionate dating, trial marriage, temporary alternative to marriage and permanent alternative to marriage

Q26 - Sue Sharpe studied working-class girls in 1970 and found their concerns were marriage, children etc. In 1990 she found girls' priorities had changed to their career and independence. Her findings could help explain the decline decrease in marriage over past 40 years because:

C – it highlighted the increasing influence of women's rights – focus on career and not being a housewife

Q27 - The number of births outside marriage has increased to around 50% of all births in 2013. One explanation for this decrease could be due to:

B – The growth in cohabitation as helped remove the stigma of births outside marriage

Q28 - women are having fewer children or having them later in life (in 2013 the average age of becoming a mother increased to 30 years) or indeed remaining childless. One explanation for this increase could be due to:

D - Beck suggests this latter change is due to the increasing contradiction between women's domestic roles and paid employment

Q29 - The number of divorces in the UK have risen sharply since the 1970s with around 42% of all marriages ending in divorce. One explanation for this could be higher expectations of marriage. Allan and Crow explains this as meaning:

A - individuals seek fulfilment from marriage and divorce if it's not found

Q30 - The number of divorces in the UK have risen sharply since the 1970s with around 42% of all marriages ending in divorce. One explanation is secularization; secularization is:

A - declining influence of religion on society

Q31 – An empty shell marriage is:

C - where a couple remains legally married but love, sex and companionship are in the past

Q32 - Marxist feminists' argue rising divorce rates are an outcome of the tensions caused by the dual-burden of capitalism. The dual-burden is:

B – where women are forced to undertake unpaid labour at home, while in the workplace they tend to occupy jobs with low wages

Q33 - Radical feminists would point out increasing divorce rates are an outcome of the dark-side of family life being more openly discussed allowing women to:

C – leave oppressive relationships as well as protecting children from witnessing violent relationships

Q34 - The term 'dark side' of the family refers to:

C - abuse within the family, particularly towards women and children

Q35 - Elizabeth Bott's 'Family and Social Network' looks at two contrasting types of conjugal roles: segregated and joint. Segregated and joint conjugal roles are:

C – Segregated conjugal roles involve a clear differentiation between the tasks undertaken by men and women. Joint conjugal roles where husband and wife share tasks with little or no differentiation between the tasks

Q36 - Wilmott and Young's 'The Symmetrical Family' detects a shift in conjugal roles moving away from traditional segregated roles towards more:

D - symmetrical forms of relationships

Q37 - Duncombe and Marsden's research reinforces previous studies revealing inequalities in power and domestic responsibilities. They coined the term the 'triple-shift' to describe the burden placed on women. The term 'triple-shift' refers to:

D – paid work outside the home, housework and emotional work

Q38 - Married women become economically dependent on their husbands especially as once children arrive women give up work in order to look after the children. Phal's research found the consequence of this on a woman's economic position within a marriage is:

B – men tended to control and manage a couple's money

Q39 - Neil Postman argues childhood is disappearing as children are able to experience things that previously were only available to adults. What term does Postman use to describe the influence of the mass media on the erosion of childhood?

C - Frankenstein Syndrome

Q40 – What do you understand by the term child-centeredness:

C – where parents put their children first

3 FAMILY - SINGLE QUESTIONS

Q1 Identify one reason why women today might delay having children

Q2 Identify one reason why the lives of children are seen to have improved over the past 100 years

Q3 Identify one reason why ethnic diversity over the past 50 years has increased family diversity

Q4 Identify one reason which illustrates how the difference between children and adults has narrowed

Q5 Identify one reason why the number of first-time marriages are in decline

Q6 Identify one reason why women might have less children than 50 years ago

Q7 Identify one reason for increasing life expectancy

Q8 Identify two effects of women undertaking paid work on a couple's relationship

Q9 Identify two changing functions of the family

Q10 Identify two features of the symmetrical family

Q11 Identify two ways in which industrialization changed the lives of children

Q12 Identify two influences which could explain the growth in family diversity

Q13 Identify two criticisms of functionalist views of the family

Q14 Identify two criticisms of Marxist views of the family

Q15 Identify two criticisms of feminist views of the family

Q16 Identify two criticisms of radical feminist views of the family

Q17 Identify four ways in which feminist sociologists have aided our understanding of family dynamics

Q18 Identify four reasons for the for the changes in family size over the past 100 years

4 **FAMILY** – SINGLE QUESTIONS: THE ANSWERS

Q1 Identify one reason why women today might delay having children

- age at which women start having a family is rising
- women are delaying starting a family to pursue a career
- rising costs mean couples prefer to save first
- the availability of IVF and other reproductive technology 'extends' the delay
- more women are going to university and other educational opportunities

Q2 Identify one reason why the lives of children are seen to have improved over the past 100 years

- improved overall health
- improved diet and nutrition
- improved health care and associated treatments
- families more child-centred
- more rights for children
- improved education opportunities

Q3 Identify one reason why ethnic diversity over the past 50 years has increased family diversity

- more extended families
- diverse attitudes to marriage
- differing parent/child relationships
- number of children in a family
- differing attitudes to divorce
- differing relationships between husband and wife

Q4 Identify one reason which illustrates how the difference between children and adults has narrowed

- children have greater access to the adult world especially via Internet
- the difference between adult and youth culture has narrowed with parents accompanying their teenage children to concerts
- aspects of social media like Facebook and Instagram are enjoyed by children and their parents for example teenagers have their parents as 'friends'
- children are increasingly economically dependent on their parents much later in life; for example children living at parental home much longer meaning the parent can still 'see' their 25 year-old offspring as a child
- lifelong learning is extending childhood for example children can now continue studying late into their twenties so the parent is still 'looking-after' their offspring

Q5 Identify one reason why the number of first-time marriages are in decline

- cohabitation has become an accepted alternative to marriage
- men are increasingly becoming fearful of divorce settlements going in a woman's favour
- some remarriages can involve people who have never married before
- less stigma associated with singlehood
- increase in divorce rates can make a couple wary of marriage

Q6 Identify one reason why women might have less children than 50 years ago

- less stigma associated with being childless
- greater career opportunities
- greater costs in bringing up children
- increased child-centredness puts a greater burden on the woman
- more availability of contraception and morning-after pill
- women defer having children to much later in life

Q7 Identify one reason for increasing life expectancy

- improved health-care facilities
- improved/better awareness of healthier diet
- improved/better awareness of health education
- improved sanitation
- improved/better awareness of available hospital treatments/medicines
- improved/better awareness of working-conditions

Q8 Identify two effects of women undertaking paid work on a couple's relationship

- gender scripts – socially constructed expectations of roles within the family could be challenged with man/husband having to do more child-care
- changing financial controls – man/husband giving up complete control
- emotional labour – child-care could become shared between husband and wife
- decision making – this could become shared between husband/wife
- divorce – added strain of wife being out at work further career could empower her to file for divorce or husband could become disgruntled and file for divorce
- expressive and instrumental roles – these could reverse with dad staying at home while wife becomes breadwinner
- dark-side of the family – wife's new role and confidence could make male partner/husband jealous and he becomes violent (domestic violence)

Q9 Identify two changing functions of the family

- social control of its members
- education
- primary and secondary socialization
- reproduction of children
- nurturing of children
- passing on property
- family was once responsible for health-care and welfare provision

24

Q10 Identify two features of the symmetrical family

- women in paid employment
- men helping with domestic/housework work such as washing-up
- couples sharing childcare
- couples sharing decision making
- couples sharing leisure time

Q11 Identify two ways in which industrialization changed the lives of children

- compulsory schooling/education means adult's responsibility for looking after their children is increasing
- children given rights in law as well as increasing child-centredness
- fall in infant mortality rates as well as birthrates means it's easier for a parent to focus their attention on one child than several (child-centredness)
- the mass media have turned their attention on children with dedicated programmes in addition mass media has narrowed the gap between adult and children's entertainment e.g. social media
- children are targeted by big business making them consumers in their own right e.g. pester-power

Q12 Identify two influences which could explain the growth in family diversity

- confluent love
- ageing population
- increasing divorce rates
- changing women's position
- gay rights movement
- secularization of society
- increasing trends in cohabitation
- increasing trends in singlehood
- social and legal recognition of same sex relations

Q13 Identify two criticisms of functionalist views of the family

- Murdock's views of the family are value laden, they are prejudicial against women and anti-family diversity
- ignores the dark-side of the family
- Willmott and Young – the extended family still exists which goes against the idea industrialization gave rise to the emergence of the nuclear family and it being geographically mobile

Q14 Identify two criticisms of Marxist views of the family

- the Marxist view that capitalism is unjust is rejected by many sociologists
- sociologists agree the family is influenced by economic system, however most disagree the family is shaped by its needs

Q15 Identify two criticisms of feminist views of the family

- feminists ignore the positive aspects of family life as many women enjoy running a home and bringing up children
- feminists ignore the rise of gender equality in areas of equal pay allowing women more say in decision making within the family
- there is evidence of greater gender equality within the home, with a small but increasing number of men becoming househusbands

Q16 Identify two criticisms of radical feminist views of the family

- some families are matriarchal as opposed to being patriarchal
- ignores the role of capitalism in oppressing women
- some men support the women's movement and its associated rights
- it ignores the advances made in women's rights on issues such as equal pay
- it ignores the class differences in women's position, the higher the social-class of women the greater their rights

Q17 Identify four ways in which feminist sociologists have aided our understanding of family dynamics

- the triple-shift
- the dual burden
- trouble free sex
- the emasculation of women through emotional responsibilities
- women's economic dependency on men
- patriarchal power on decision making

Q18 Identify four reasons for the for the changes in family size over the past 100 years

- geographic mobility
- influence of feminism
- dual-worker households
- child-centredness
- cost of raising children
- changes in infant mortality
- changes in social policy on welfare payments
- contraception
- changing role of women

5 **EDUCATION** - MULTIPLE CHOICE QUESTIONS

Q1 The 1944 Education Act established 3 types of schools. This system was known as:

A – the triple system

B- marketization system

C – the tripartite system

D – the post-war system

Q2 The 1944 Education Act established particular types of schools:

A – public schools; fee-paying schools and independent schools

B – Free Schools; Academy Schools and Specialist Schools

C – state schools; comprehensive and Grammar Schools

D – secondary modern schools; secondary technical schools; Grammar Schools

Q3 Comprehensive schools are school which have:

A – no selection test

B – a selection test

C – the 11+ test

D – selection based on parental income

Q4 Comprehensive schools were introduced in order to:

A - reduce social class divisions and break-down social-class barriers

B – increase class divisions and construct social-class barriers

C – reduce social class barriers and introduce marketization of education

D – increase social class barriers and eliminate the marketization of education

Q5 - The 1988 Education Reform Act introduced:

A - competition between schools and turned parents into 'consumers' of education

B – competition between fee-paying schools and turned parents into 'consumers' of education

C – the post-code lottery so schools would compete with each other

D – removed the post-code lottery so schools would no longer compete with each other

Q6 – The 1988 Education Act introduced several educational polices. Three of these are:

A - Comprehensive schools: Ofsted and open enrolment and parental choice

B - Grammar Schools; secondary modern schools and the tripartite system

C - National Curriculum; Ofsted: open enrolment and parental choice

D - secondary modern schools; secondary technical schools; Grammar Schools

Q7 – Writing over 100 years' ago Durkheim argued the main function of education was to bind members of society together. Therefore the education system is:

A – a social adhesive

B - a dysfunctional perquisite

C - a function of society

D – a functional perquisite

Q8 For functionalists one of the key functions of the education system is:

A – to cultivate ascribed status

B – to cultivate achieved status

C – to nurture primary socialization

D – to prevent meritocracy

Q9 - Althusser (Marxist) argued that the main role of education in a capitalist society was the reproduction of:

A - an anti-meritocratic ideology

B – anti-school subcultures

C – an efficient and obedient work force

D – an inefficient and disobedient work force

Q10 – Bowles and Gintis (Marxists) came up with the concept of 'the correspondence principle'. The correspondence principle recognizes:

A - a school's processes are very dissimilar to offices and factories

B - schools legitimate the myth that everyone has an equal chance

C - school processes recognize the myth of meritocracy

D - a school's processes are very similar to those found in offices and factories

Q11 Both functionalist and Marxist perspectives have similarities. They both:

A - tend to ignore social processes within school – except Willis

B - tend to ignore social processes outside school – except Willis

C - tend to ignore social processes in and outside school – except Willis

D - tend to ignore social processes within school – except Willis

Q12 – Which term does Bourdieu use to describe the cultural characteristics and values of each social class?

A – deviancy amplification

B – habitus

C- myth of meritocracy

D - counter-culture

Q13 – Cultural capital as identified by Bourdieu refers to:

A – pupil premium

B – deferred gratification

C – the knowledge, language and values which readily translate into educational capital

D – present time orientation

Q14 – Cultural differences are extended further by examining sub-cultural differences between social groups. Sugarman and Hyman highlighted the effects of socialization because:

A – the middle classes socialized their children to have present time orientation and deferred gratification

B - the middle classes socialized their children to have future time orientation and immediate gratification

C - the middle classes socialized their children to have present time orientation and immediate gratification

D - the middle classes socialized their children to have future time orientation and deferred gratification

Q15 – Bernstein's research focused on linguistic deprivation and is influence on educational success. Bernstein distinguished between:

A – academic speeches codes and non-academic speech codes

B – educational speech codes and vocational speech codes

C – restricted speech codes and elaborated speech codes

D – compensatory speech codes and pupil premium speech codes

Q16 – Pupil premium is used by the state as a form of:

A – compensatory education

B – fatalism

C – homework policy

D – streaming

Q17 - Rutter places great emphasis on the way a school organizes itself. The better their organizational structures and polices the better the school. Three of these policies are:

A – streaming; setting and assemblies

B- setting; homework policy; and sports day

C - marking policy; teacher reward systems; mixed ability classes

D – mixed ability classes; Maths lessons; English lessons

Q18 – Bowles and Ginitis talk of the myth of meritocracy. The myth of meritocracy refers to:

A – schools make sure all students are aware only a select number of people will ever succeed

B – schools tell students failure is a myth

C - schools legitimate the myth that everyone has an equal chance

D – schools tell children if you work hard your dreams will come true

Q19 – The difference between setting and streaming is:

A - setting is where pupils of <u>similar</u> ability are put in different sets (groups) in <u>specific</u> subjects studied, while streaming involves grouping students of <u>similar</u> ability for <u>every</u> subject studied

B – setting is where pupils of <u>different</u> ability are put in different groups/sets in <u>some</u> subjects studied, while streaming involves grouping students of <u>similar</u> ability for <u>every</u> subject studied

C - setting is where pupils of <u>similar</u> ability are put in different groups/sets in specific subjects studied, while streaming involves grouping students of <u>different</u> ability for <u>every</u> subject studied

D - setting is where pupils of different ability are put in different groups/sets in <u>some</u> subjects studied, while streaming involves grouping students of <u>similar</u> ability for <u>some</u> subject studied

Q20 – The halo effect is positive stereotype given by teachers to pupils who:

A – are seen as lazy and troublesome

B – have a 'culture of resistance' to school life

C – are enthusiastic and hardworking

D - form anti-school subcultures

Q21 - Rosenthal and Jacobson's (1968) research found positive and negative labels helped produce:

A – mixed ability classes

B – self-fulfilling prophecy in the classroom

C – material deprivation

D – setting and streaming

Q22 - Mac an Ghaill (1994) identified 3 working-class male subcultures. These are:

A – macho lads; macho lasses; macho people

B – bright lads; average lads; slow lads

C – academic achievers; average achievers; low achievers

D - macho lads; academic achievers; new enterprisers

Q23 – As well as Paul Willis, Colin Lacey's (1970) study of Hightown Grammar school also showed how streaming can lead to the creation of:

A – halo effect

B – anti-school subculture

C – meritocracy

D – cultural capital

Q24 - C. Jackson (2006) 'Lads and Ladettes in School: Gender and the Fear of Failure' looked at how girls are forming anti-school subcultures and becoming:

A – ladettes because of the fear of boys

B – ladettes because of the fear of academic success

C – ladettes because of the fear of academic failure

D - ladettes because of the fear of PE

Q25 – Complete the sentence: 'Gender is not the strongest predictor of attainment…..'

A – because social class attainment gap at Key Stage 4 is three times as wide as the gender gap and some minority ethnic groups achievement is much greater than the gap between boys and girls.

B – because social class attainment gap at Key Stage 4 is insignificant but some minority ethnic groups achievement is much greater than the gap between boys and girls.

C - because social class attainment gap at Key Stage 4 is three times as wide as the gender gap and some minority ethnic groups achievement is insignificant compared to the gap between boys and girls.

D - because social class attainment gap and some minority ethnic groups achievement is the same as than the gap between boys and girls.

Q26 - Teacher-pupil interaction affecting the gender gap. Howe (1997) identified the different ways teachers interact with boys and girls - such differences in interaction emerge….

A – late, around Key Stage 4

B – very late, around Key Stage 5

C - very early, even in preschool

D – early, even in Key Stage 2

Q27 - Masculine identity can be seen as incompatible with academic success. Kelly (1987) found science and the science classroom remain:

A – gender neutral environments with either gender of teacher dominating science classrooms

B – gender neutral environments with nobody dominating science classrooms

C – 'feminine' environments with girls dominating science classrooms

D - 'masculine' environments with boys dominating science classrooms

Q28 – The term ethnocentric curriculum refers to:

A – the school curriculum and the hidden curriculum is too focused on white British culture and adds to the low self-esteem and underachievement of ethnic minorities

B – the school curriculum and the hidden curriculum is not focused enough on white British culture and adds to the low self-esteem and underachievement of ethnic minorities

C – the hidden curriculum is too focused on white British culture and adds to the low self-esteem and underachievement of ethnic minorities

D - school curriculum is too focused on white British culture and adds to the low self-esteem and underachievement of ethnic minorities

Q29 – Family life outside school can affect achievement inside school. Some minority ethnic groups have stronger parental support than others. Chinese students are seen to have high levels of achievement in school because:

A – Archer (2006) found Chinese students and parents put a high value on education as it gave the family a high standing in their community

B- Archer (2006) found Chinese students and parents put a low value on education as it gave the family a high standing in their community

C - Archer (2006) found Chinese students and parents were indifferent to education as it gave the family a high standing in their community

D - Archer (2006) found Chinese students and parents put a high value on education as it gave the family a no standing in their community

Q30 - Ethnicity and achievement. Identify which of the three statements is correct:

A - Stephen J. Ball (2008) found that Black Caribbean and African students are more likely to be identified for gifted and talented programmes. In contrast, evidence also suggests that Chinese and Indian students are less likely to be entered into higher sets

B - Stephen J. Ball (2008) found that Black Caribbean and African students are less likely to be identified for gifted and talented programmes. Evidence also suggests that Chinese and Indian students are also likely to be entered into lower sets

Continues overleaf

C - Stephen J. Ball (2008) found that Black Caribbean and African students are more likely to be identified for gifted and talented programmes. In addition, evidence also suggests that Chinese and Indian students are more likely to be entered into higher sets

D - Stephen J. Ball (2008) found that Black Caribbean and African students are less likely to be identified for gifted and talented programmes. In contrast, evidence also suggests that Chinese and Indian students are more likely to be entered into higher sets

Q31 – Ethnicity and achievement. Identify which of the three statements is correct:

A - African-Caribbean and Bangladeshi Asians are less likely to be working-class and not in poverty and so have a general material advantage while Indian and African Asian children are more likely to come from professional/business middle-class backgrounds and the subsequent advantages

B - African-Caribbean and Bangladeshi Asians are more likely to be working-class and in poverty and so have a general material disadvantage while Indian and African Asian children are more likely to come from professional/business middle-class backgrounds and the subsequent advantages

C - African-Caribbean and Bangladeshi Asians are more likely to be working-class as are Indian and African Asian children and have a general material disadvantage

D - African-Caribbean and Bangladeshi Asians and Indian and African Asian children are more likely to come from professional/business middle-class backgrounds and the subsequent material advantages

Q32 Ethnicity and attainment. Identify which of the three statements is correct:

A - some ethnic groups, such as Chinese students, have far higher levels of attainment compared to the national level

B – some ethnic groups, such as Chinese students, have far lower levels of attainment compared to the national level

C – some ethnic groups, such as Chinese students, have average levels of attainment compared to the national level

Q33 – Ethnicity and attainment. Identify which of the three statements is correct:

A - Chinese students are the highest attaining group, with 95.5% achieving 5 A*-C grades including Maths and English. This compares to 70% in 2006/07

B - Chinese students are the lowest attaining group, with 38.5% achieving 5 A*-C grades including Maths and English. This compares to 70% in 2006/07

C - Chinese students are the highest attaining group, with 78.5% achieving 5 A*-C grades including Maths and English. This compares to 70% in 2006/07

Q34 - Ethnicity and attainment. Identify which of the four statements is correct:

A - Bangladeshi pupils now have a slightly lower attainment rate than White pupils, with 59.7% 5 A*-C grades including Maths and English. This is a massive improvement given that only around 40% achieved this 2006/07, which was 5% less than White pupils

B - Bangladeshi pupils now have a slightly higher attainment rate than White pupils, with 99.7% 5 A*-C grades including Maths and English. This is a massive improvement given that only around 40% achieved this 2006/07, which was 5% less than White pupils

C - Bangladeshi pupils now have a slightly higher attainment rate than White pupils, with 59.7% 5 A*-C grades including Maths and English. This is a massive improvement given that only around 40% achieved this 2006/07, which was 5% less than White pupils

Q35 – Ethnicity and attainment. Identify which of the four statements is correct:

A - Travellers, Gypsies and Roma are still the highest achieving groups, with 97.5% of Irish Travellers and 90.8% of those from Gypsy or Roma backgrounds achieving 5 A*-C grades including Maths and English.

B - Travellers, Gypsies and Roma are still the lowest achieving groups, with 17.5% of Irish Travellers and 10.8% of those from Gypsy or Roma backgrounds achieving 5 A*-C grades including Maths and English.

C - Travellers, Gypsies and Roma are still the average achieving groups, with 47.5% of Irish Travellers and 50.8% of those from Gypsy or Roma backgrounds achieving 5 A*-C grades including Maths and English.

6 EDUCATION - MULTIPLE CHOICE ANSWERS

Q1 The 1944 Education Act established 3 types of schools. This system was known as:

C – the tripartite system

Q2 The 1944 Education Act established particular types of schools:

D – secondary modern schools; secondary technical schools; grammar schools

Q3 Comprehensive schools are schools which have:

A – no selection test

Q4 Comprehensive schools were introduced in order to

A - reduce social class divisions and break-down social-class barriers

Q5 - The 1988 Education Reform Act introduced

A - competition between schools turning parents into 'consumers' of education

Q6 – The 1988 Education Act introduced several educational polices. Three of these are:

C - National Curriculum; Ofsted: open enrolment and parental choice

Q7 – Writing over 100 years' ago Durkheim argued the main function of education was to bind members of society together. Therefore the education system is

D – a functional perquisite

Q8 For functionalists one of the key functions of the education system is

B – to cultivate achieved status

Q9 - Althusser (Marxist) argued that the main role of education in a capitalist society was the reproduction of

C – an efficient and obedient work force

Q10 – Bowles and Gintis (Marxists) came up with the concept of 'the correspondence principle'. The correspondence principle recognizes

D - a school's processes as being very similar to those found in offices and factories

Q11 Both functionalist and Marxist perspectives have similarities. They both

A - tend to ignore social processes within school – except Willis

Q12 – Which term does Bourdieu use to describe the cultural characteristics and values of each social class?

B – habitus

Q13 – Cultural capital as identified by Bourdieu refers to:

C – the knowledge, language and values which readily translate into educational capital

Q14 – Cultural differences are extended further by examining sub-cultural differences between social groups. Sugarman and Hyman highlighted the effects of socialization because:

D - the middle classes socialized their children to have future time orientation and deferred gratification

Q15 – Bernstein's research focused on linguistic deprivation and its influence on educational success. Bernstein distinguished between:

C – restricted speech codes and elaborated speech codes

Q16 – Pupil premium is used by the state as a form of:

A – compensatory education

Q17 - Rutter places great emphasis on the way a school organizes itself. The better their organizational structures and polices the better the school. Three of these policies are:

C - marking policy; teacher reward systems; mixed ability classes

Q18 – Bowles and Ginitis talk of the myth of meritocracy. The myth of meritocracy refers to:

C - schools legitimate the myth that everyone has an equal chance

Q19 – The difference between setting and streaming is:

A - setting is where pupils of <u>similar</u> ability are put in different sets (groups) in <u>specific</u> subjects studied, while streaming involves grouping students of <u>similar</u> ability for <u>every</u> subject studied

Q20 – The halo effect is positive stereotype given by teachers to pupils who

C – are enthusiastic and hardworking

Q21 - Rosenthal and Jacobson's (1968) research found positive and negative labels helped produce

B – self-fulfilling prophecy in the classroom

Q22 - Mac an Ghaill (1994) identified 3 working-class male subcultures

D - macho lads; academic achievers; new enterprisers

Q23 – As well as Paul Willis, Colin Lacey's (1970) study of Hightown Grammar school also showed how streaming can lead to the creation of

B – anti-school subculture

Q24 - C. Jackson (2006) 'Lads and Ladettes in School: Gender and the Fear of Failure' looked at how girls are forming anti-school subcultures and becoming

C – ladettes because of the fear of academic failure

Q25 – Complete the sentence: 'Gender is not the strongest predictor of attainment…..'

A – because social class attainment gap at Key Stage 4 is three times as wide as the gender gap and some minority ethnic groups achievement is much greater than the gap between boys and girls.

Q26 - Teacher-pupil interaction affecting the gender gap. Howe (1997) identified the different ways teachers interact with boys and girls - such differences in interaction emerge….

C - very early, even in preschool

Q27 - Masculine identity can be seen as incompatible with academic success. Kelly (1987) found science and the science classroom remain

D - 'masculine' environments with boys dominating science classrooms

Q28 – The term ethnocentric curriculum refers to

A – the school curriculum and the hidden curriculum is too focused on white British culture and adds to the low self-esteem and underachievement of ethnic minorities

Q29 – Family life outside school can affect achievement inside school. Some minority ethnic groups have stronger parental support than others. Chinese students are seen to have high levels of achievement in school because

A – Archer (2006) found Chinese students and parents put a high value on education as it gave the family a high standing in their community

Q30 - Ethnicity and achievement. Highlight which of the following four statements is correct:

D - Stephen J. Ball (2008) found that Black Caribbean and African students are less likely to be identified for gifted and talented programmes. In contrast, evidence also suggests that Chinese and Indian students are more likely to be entered into higher sets

Q31 – Ethnicity and achievement. Highlight which of the following three statements is correct:

B - African-Caribbean and Bangladeshi Asians are more likely to be working-class and in poverty and so have a general material disadvantage while Indian and African Asian children are more likely to come from professional/business middle-class backgrounds and the subsequent advantages

Q32 Ethnicity and attainment. Identify which of the three statements is correct.

A - some ethnic groups, such as Chinese students, have far higher levels of attainment compared to the national level

Q33 – Ethnicity and attainment. Identify which of the three statements is correct.

C - Chinese students are the highest attaining group, with 78.5% achieving 5 A*-C grades including Maths and English. This compares to 70% in 2006/07

Q34 - Ethnicity and attainment. Identify which of the three statements is correct:

C - Bangladeshi pupils now have a slightly higher attainment rate than White pupils, with 59.7% 5 A*-C grades including Maths and English. This is a massive improvement given that only around 40% achieved this 2006/07, which was 5% less than White pupils

Q35 – Ethnicity and attainment. Identify which of the three statements is correct:

B - Travellers, Gypsies and Roma are still the lowest achieving groups, with 17.5% of Irish Travellers and 10.8% of those from Gypsy or Roma backgrounds achieving 5 A*-C grades including Maths and English.

7 **EDUCATION** - SINGLE QUESTIONS

Q1 Identify two reasons why are girls have higher levels of achievement in school than boys

Q2 Identify two reasons why girls have high levels of achievement in school (this question doesn't mention boys)

Q3 Identify two reasons why boys are underachieving in school (this question makes no mention of girls)

Q4 Identify two functions that the education system might perform

Q5 Identify two polices contributing to the marketization of education

Q6 Identify two ways in which cultural deprivation might affect work-class pupil under achievement in school (this question is not asking about material factors)

Q7 Functionalists have their own perspective on the purpose of the education system. Identify two criticisms other sociologists might make of the functionalist perspective.

Q8 Identify three ways in which social policies may have influenced social-class differences in educational achievement

Q9 Identify three factors outside school which may have aided girls' achievement in school (you do not mention factors inside school)

Q10 Identify three factors within schools which may have affect the educational underachievement of some ethnic minority groups.

Q11 – Identify three ways in which Marxists would say the education system and its processes replicate the workplace.

Q12 – Identify three types of school subcultures

Q13 – Identify three reasons why working-class parents might not attend parents' evenings

Q14 - Identify three processes inside school which may have an effect on pupils from different social groups

Q15 - Identify three processes outside school which may have an effect on pupils from different social groups

Q16 – identify one criticism of labelling theory

Q17 – Identify three ways in which a school's curriculum might be ethnocentric

Q18 – Identify two policies designed to encourage the introduction of market forces in the education system

Q19 – Identify two ways in which pupils identities might be shaped by their experiences at school

8 **EDUCATION** - SINGLE QUESTIONS: THE ANSWERS

Q1 Identify two reasons why are girls have higher levels of achievement in school than boys

- the women's movement and feminism raised girls' expectations and self-esteem
- the increasing number of employment opportunities for women
- many girls' mother are in paid employment and act as positive role models for them
- girls' priorities have changed: Sue Sharpe (1976) 'Just Like a Girl'
- girls are better motivated and organised than boys
- girls at 16 are seen to be more mature than boys
- girls benefitted from introduction of coursework in GCSEs/A-Levels
- national curriculum made more subjects compulsory
- teachers less likely to gender stereotype girls into set roles or careers

Q2 Identify two reasons why girls have high levels of achievement in school (this question doesn't mention boys)

- the women's movement and feminism raised girls' expectations and self-esteem
- the increasing number of employment opportunities for women
- many girls' mother are in paid employment and act as positive role models for them
- girls' priorities have changed: Sue Sharpe (1976) 'Just Like a Girl'

Q3 Identify two reasons why boys are underachieving in school (this question makes no mention of girls)

- boys are generally more disruptive in class than girls
- boys appear to gain 'street cred' by not working hard
- decline in traditional male jobs
- teachers tend to have lower expectations of boys
- lack of male role models in schools
- laddish subcultures
- identity crisis in men – uncertain future removes purpose in achieving
- boys do not like reading as it has become feminised
- boys tend to overestimate their ability
- feminisation of assessment – coursework rather than competitive exams

Q4 Identify two functions that the education system might perform

- secondary socialization
- gender role socialization
- division of labour
- role allocation
- establishment of universalistic values
- meritocracy
- value consensus through the hidden curriculum
- meritocracy
- competition

Q5 Identify two polices contributing to the marketization of education

- publication of school league tables showing exam results
- schools competing for pupils
- publication of Ofsted reports
- schools opting out of local authority control
- encouragement of different types of schools - Free Schools; Academies etc
- 1988 Education Reform Act

Q6 Identify two ways in which cultural deprivation might affect work-class pupil under achievement in school (this question is not asking about material factors)

- immediate gratification
- present time orientation
- lack of cultural capital
- parental attitudes to education
- sense of fatalism
- speech and language codes
- parents level of educational achievement

Q7 Functionalists have their own perspective on the purpose of the education system. Identify two criticisms other sociologists might make of the functionalist perspective.

- Marxists point out meritocracy is a myth
- Marxists would point out to functionalists how the role allocation of jobs is not conducted via meritocracy as many jobs are allocated via social-class background
- Marxists would point out to functionalists how the education system does not encourage the sharing of values through consensual processes rather the education system is there to promote a ruling-class ideology
- Paul Willis' would point out how a number of pupils reject the values being taught via the educations system. Instead of passively accepting what is being delivered/communicated they reject it and can form anti-school subcultures

- Feminists would point out the school system encourages gender role allocation eg too few girls choose to study engineering
- Feminists would point out the school system encourages patriarchal gender regimes e.g. many school leadership teams are male dominated

Q8 Identify three ways in which social policies may have influenced social-class differences in educational achievement

- Parental power as consumers of education – sometimes known as parentocracy
- New vocationalism
- Free school meals
- Compensatory education policies
- Correspondence principle
- Expansion of Higher Education
- Marketization
- Private schooling

Q9 Identify three factors outside school which may have aided girls' achievement in school (you do not mention factors inside school)

- Women in paid employment
- Feminism
- Parental encouragement
- Equal opportunities in the workplace – career and pay
- Changing nature of work – more feminized jobs
- Changing patterns of work – more flexible shift work allowing women to balance child-care with paid work
- Increase in divorce rates
- Increase in lone parenting
- Changing girls aspirations
- Different leisure patterns – girls prefer reading/conversation improving their linguistic skills needed for literature based subjects. Much of this comes from be socialized by their mothers reading to them as children

Q10 Identify three factors within schools which may have affect the educational underachievement of some ethnic minority groups.

- self-fulfilling prophecy from teacher labelling
- teacher's negativity
- teacher racism
- ethnocentric curriculum
- discriminatory admission and selection processes
- institutional racism
- anti-school subcultures
- culture of resistance – Hall

Q11 – Identify three ways in which Marxists would say the education system and its processes replicate the workplace.

- Hierarchy of authority
- Correspondence principle
- Both driven by competitive processes
- Class alienation – working class feel alienated in a predominantly middle-class institution
- Status difference – wealthy children go to fee-paying schools (end up having high-flying careers)) while the majority attend state schools (end up having jobs with limited opportunities)
- Reward systems – schools reward good work with 'stars' & 'merits' which is replicated in work-place to relieve the monotony
- Fragmented timetable learning – work – break-time – back to work – break-time – back to work

Q12 – Identify three types of school subcultures

- Male anti-school subcultures
- Female school subcultures
- African-Caribbean male subcultures
- African-Caribbean female subcultures

Q13 – Identify three reasons why working-class parents might not attend parents' evenings

- Lack of interest
- Feeling of inferiority against predominantly middle-class teachers
- More likely to be on shift-work than middle-class parents
- Having to work longer hours to compensate for low pay
- Can't afford child-minder in order to attend
- Lack of education themselves so unable to understand subject based targets set by the teacher

Q14 - Identify three processes inside school which may have an effect on pupils from different social groups

- Labelling
- Halo effect
- Self-fulfilling prophecy
- Ethnocentric curriculum
- Setting/streaming
- Mixed ability classes
- Subcultures
- School organization
- Gender regimes
- Open enrolment

Q15 - Identify three processes outside school which may have an effect on pupils from different social groups

- Material deprivation
- Cultural deprivation
- Speech codes

- Parental interest
- Parental education
- Parental occupation
- Cultural capital – habitus
- Compensatory education
- Marketization – choosing school via income – postcode lottery

Q16 – identify one criticism of labelling theory

- Too deterministic – some pupils remove the labels through hard work
- Ignores other influences – e.g. material deprivation
- Doesn't consider the influence of wider society in the construction of labels given out in classroom e.g. race
- Assumes pupils are aware they have been labelled – some aren't
- Assumes there's always a self-fulfilling prophecy – some pupils ignore the label

Q17 – Identify three ways in which a school's curriculum might be ethnocentric

- Not providing Halal meals
- History lesson too focused on White history
- School holidays constructed around Christian calendar
- Religious assemblies delivered from a singular religious perspective
- Uniform and dress codes designed around Western values
- Dress/changing rooms for PE and Games lessons structured around Western values

Q18 – Identify two policies designed to encourage the introduction of market forces in the education system

- The National Curriculum
- National testing (SATS)
- National league tables
- Open enrolment and parental choice
- Ofsted
- Local management of schools
- Schools having control of their own admissions criteria
- Schools having their own discipline and exclusion criteria

Q19 – Identify two ways in which pupils identities might be shaped by their experiences at school

- Subject choice – though national curriculum aimed to limit differences between gender regimes in subject choice physics, chemistry and Maths are still seen as male subjects while art, English and dance are seen as girl subjects
- Gender socialization – gender stereotypes were still found in many school books
- Gender socialization - masculine identity can be seen as incompatible with academic success
- Pupil subcultures
- Teacher-pupil interaction affecting the gender gap
- Differing rates of achievement – girls outperforming boys due to wider social changes
- feminization of assessment – coursework rather than competitive exams
- gendered language
- women in the curriculum

9 RESEARCH METHODS - MULTIPLE CHOICE QUESTIONS

Q1 - Positivists prefer to collect quantitative data through the following research methods which are seen to collect reliable data

A - Informal interviews; open-ended questionnaires; data from diaries

B - Data from diaries and letters; informal interviews; open-ended questionnaires;

C- Laboratory experiments; social surveys; structured questionnaires; use of official statistics

D - Participant and non-participant observations

Q2 - Interpretivists use the term verstehen to describe their data gathering processes. Verstehen means:

A – achieving an empathetic understanding of people by seeing the world from their perspective

B – achieving an empathetic understanding of people by recording their gender, age, sexuality and ethnicity

C – achieving an empathetic understanding of people by giving them a structured questionnaire to complete

D – asking people to complete a postal questionnaire within a designated period of time

Q3 – The difference between primary and secondary sources of data is…

A – Primary data collected by sociologists themselves while secondary data is data which already exists such as that found in newspapers, novels etc.

B – Secondary data collected by sociologists themselves while primary data is data which already exists such as that found in newspapers, novels etc.

C – Primary data is collect first and secondary data is collected second.

D – Primary data is quantitative sources and secondary data is qualitative sources

Q4 - When doing research sociologists always consider the ethics of what they are doing because

A – sociologists are 'right-on' sort of people

B – sociologists are concerned with morality (what is right and wrong) when undertaking research

C – sociologists are seeking the truth through research methods

D – sociologists are concerned about getting to the truth through any means possible

Q5 – When sociologists talk about validity they are concerned with:

A – their chosen method is repeatable

B – their chosen method is ethical

C – their chosen method being representative

D – their chosen method uncovering the truth

Q6 – When sociologists talk about a sampling-frame they are referring to:

A - the whole group being studied

B – a type of sample method select from which to draw their data

C – where they will gather their data in order to make certain it is a representative sample

D - a list of names of all those included in the survey population from which the sample is selected

Q7 – A representative sample is

A – is chosen from a subdivided group of people e.g. a specific age range in order to cover a reasonable cross-section of the group being surveyed

B – selects people at random in order to cover a reasonable cross-section of the group being surveyed

C - is a smaller group taken from the population being surveyed in to cover a reasonable cross-section of the group being surveyed

D – is about selecting from the sampling frame at regular intervals until the size of sample is reached

Q8 – When sociologists conduct social surveys they usually use

A – open interviews and observations

B – a unique sampling method

C – questionnaires or structured interviews

D – a unique research method

Q9 – When sociologists conduct field experiments they

A – carry them out in the real world conditions, such as a school, while at the same time trying to follow similar procedures to those found in any laboratory experiment

B – carry them out on school playing fields or similar surroundings, while at the same time trying to follow similar procedures to those found in any laboratory experiment

C – carry them out in the real world conditions, such as a school, while at the same time trying not to follow similar procedures to those found in any laboratory experiment

D - carry them out on school playing fields or similar surroundings, while at the same time trying not to follow similar procedures to those found in any laboratory experiment

Q10 – One problem of using the experimental method in sociology is

A – the Hawthorne Effect

B- the sample method

C – the comparative method

D – the viral effect

Q11 – Which type of sociologists prefer to use the social survey method?

A – interpretivists

B – field experimentalists

C – positivists

D – qualitativists

Q12 – Social surveys cause three distinct problems for sociologists

A – validity, generalisation, reliability

B – validity, replicability, desirability

C – validity, ethics, replicability

D – validity, victimology, methodology

Q13 When sociologists' talk of the imposition problem, they are referring to:

A – the limited availability of respondents imposing artificial limits on the data available for collection

B – the limited availability of prepared questions imposing artificial limits on the data available for collection

C – the limited choice of answers imposing artificial limits on the data available for collection

D – the limited amount of time available to the respondent imposing artificial limits on the data available for collection

Q14 – Pre-coded questionnaires are those with

A – have no structure

B – leave the respondent free to complete in a manner they feel appropriate

C – are highly structured

D – leave enough room for the respondent to write the minimum of two sentences

Q15 – Postal questionnaires are

A – tend to be sent through the post to the respondent

B – tend to left at the Post-Office for the respondent to collect

C – tend to be sent through the post to the respondent along with a pre-paid addressed envelope

D – are no longer used by sociologists due to the rising cost of postage

Q16 One problem with postal questionnaires is

A – not enough respondents collect them from the Post-Office to make the survey results valid and representative

B – you can't ask any embarrassing questions

C – because there's a return-envelope the sociologists gets more data than they can process

D – there is never any way of knowing who completed the questionnaire causing major problems for the validity and representativeness of the results

Q17 – One problem with the validity of research conducted through the use of open - questionnaires is:

A – they are quick to repeat

B – participant observations are more valid

C – they produce reliable data

D – the range of answers can be so broad they're difficult to quantify

Q18 – Content analysis involves:

A – involves the analysis of 'messages' in mass media content such as TV programmes, newspapers, magazines etc (secondary sources) which can generate both quantitative and qualitative data

B - involves the analysis of 'messages' of just TV (secondary sources) content which can generate both quantitative and qualitative data

C - involves the analysis of 'messages' of just newspaper content (secondary sources) which can generate both quantitative and qualitative data

D - involves the analysis of 'messages' in mass media content such as TV programmes, newspapers, magazines etc (secondary sources) which can generate only qualitative data

Q 19 One weakness of conducting content analysis is

A - Low cost

B - Time consuming

C - Can make comparisons over time (longitudinal study)

D - Quantitative analysis is seen as reliable

Q 20 - Triangulation sometimes referred to as methodological pluralism is

A – the formation of a triangular structure from quantitative data in order to assess the validity of a method

B – the formation of triangular structure from qualitative data in order to assess the validity of a method

C - is the use of one or more research method when carrying out social research in order for the different methods to complement each other

D - is the use of one or more research method when carrying out social research in order for the different methods to challenge each other

Q21 – Overt observations is where

A - the researcher will disclose themselves to the participants so they know they're being observed

B – the researcher hides themselves from the participants so they don't know they're being observed

C – the researcher participates in what they're observing

D – the researcher doesn't participate in what they're observing

Q22 – When a researcher says their method is reliable they mean

A – their chosen method is concerned with seeking the truth

B – their chosen method is concerned about what is right or wrong in the research process

C – their chosen method means if another researcher conducted the same method with the same respondents they would achieve the same results

D – their chosen method is collecting primary data because it is more valid

Q23 – Longitudinal studies are studies which are:

A – conducted at regular interval with a small sample

B – conducted at regular intervals over a short period of time

C – conducted at regular intervals over a long period of time

D – conducted at regular intervals over a moderate period of time

Q24 Secondary qualitative data, is data which

A – already exists such as official statistics like crime rates

B – has to be gathered by the researchers such as through interviews

C – has to be gathered on a longitudinal basis such as school league tables

D – already exists such as diary entries

Q25 – Positivists question the reliability of participant observation because

A – they are easy to replicate and subsequently check the validity of any findings

B – they are difficult to replicate and so check the validity of any findings

C – they are difficult to replicate and subsequently improves the validity of any findings

D – they are not interested in replication

Q26 – Ethnographic studies are

A – are seen as valid as the research is conducted in a laboratory setting

B – are seen as valid as the research is conducted using closed questionnaires

C- are seen as valid as the research is conducted in a natural setting

D – are seen as valid as the research is conducted using structured interviews

Q27 – Case studies usually involve the use of

A – the experimental method particularly field experiments

B – positivist methods such as structured interviews or closed questionnaires

C - interpretivist methods such as open-interviews or participant observations

D – content analysis involving the analysis of media messages

Q28 – Triangulation can be referred to as

A – methodological ambiguity

B – methodological determinism

C – methodological singularity

D – methodological pluralism

Q29 – Longitudinal studies are studies which

A – collect data regularly once a week

B – collect data at regular intervals over a period of years

C – collect data at regular periods over a month

D – collect data at regular periods over a year

Q30 – There are three types of experiments sociologists can use

A – the laboratory, field and clandestine experiment

B – the laboratory, field and open experiment

C – the laboratory, field and natural experiment

D - the laboratory, field and closed experiment

Q31 – Field experiments are those which

A – occur in school playing fields while trying to follow similar procedures to those found in any laboratory experiment

B- occur in real-life conditions such as a school while trying to follow similar procedures to those found in any laboratory experiment

C - occur in real-life conditions such as a school while trying to follow similar procedures to those found in all sociological research

D - occur in real-life conditions such as a school while trying to follow similar procedures to those found in all social science research

Q32 – One criticism of official statistics is they are sometimes

A – massaged by the sociologist in order to avoid embarrassment if they have done something wrong

B – they are too complex to put into readable graphs or charts

C – massaged by the state to avoid embarrassing the government of the day

D – they are not in-depth enough to be put into readable graphs or charts

10 **RESEARCH METHODS** - MULTIPLE CHOICE ANSWERS

Q1 - Positivists prefer to collect quantitative data through the following research methods which are seen to collect reliable data

C- Laboratory experiments; social surveys; structured questionnaires; use of official statistics

Q2 - Interpretivists use the term verstehen to describe their data gathering processes. Verstehen means:

A – achieving an empathetic understanding of people by seeing the world from their perspective

Q3 – The difference between primary and secondary sources of data is...

A – Primary data collected by sociologists themselves while secondary data is data which already exists such as that found in newspapers, novels etc.

Q4 - When doing research sociologists always consider the ethics of what they are doing because

B – sociologists are concerned with morality (what is right and wrong) when undertaking research

Q5 – When sociologists talk about validity they are concerned with:

D – their chosen method uncovering the truth

Q6 – When sociologists talk about a sampling-frame they are referring to:

D - a list of names of all those included in the survey population from which the sample is selected

Q7 – A representative sample is

C - is a smaller group taken from the population being surveyed in to cover a reasonable cross-section of the group being surveyed

Q8 – When sociologists conduct social surveys they usually use

C – questionnaires or structured interviews

Q9 – When sociologists conduct field experiments they

A – carry them out in the real world conditions, such as a school, while at the same time trying to follow similar procedures to those found in any laboratory experiment

Q10 – One problem of using the experimental method in sociology is

A – the Hawthorne Effect

Q11 – Which type of sociologists prefer to use the social survey method?

C – positivists

Q12 – Social surveys cause three distinct problems for sociologists

A – validity, generalization, reliability

Q13 When sociologists' talk of the imposition problem, they are referring to:

C – the limited choice of answers imposing artificial limits on the data available for collection

Q14 – Pre-coded questionnaires are those with

C – are highly structured

Q15 – Postal questionnaires are

C – tend to be sent through the post to the respondent along with a pre-paid addressed envelope

Q16 One problem with postal questionnaires is

D – there is never any way of knowing who completed the questionnaire causing major problems for the validity and representativeness of the results

Q17 – One problem with the validity of research conducted through the use of open - questionnaires is:

D – the range of answers can be so broad they're difficult to quantify

Q18 – Content analysis involves:

A – involves the analysis of 'messages' in mass media content such as TV programmes, newspapers, magazines etc (secondary sources) which can generate both quantitative and qualitative data

Q 19 One weakness of conducting content analysis is

B - Time consuming

Q 20 - Triangulation sometimes referred to as methodological pluralism is

C - is the use of one or more research method when carrying out social research in order for the different methods to complement each other

Q21 – Overt observations is where

A - the researcher will disclose themselves to the participants so they know they're being observed

Q22 – When a researcher says their method is reliable they mean

C – their chosen method means if another researcher conducted the same method with the same respondents they would achieve the same results

Q23 – Longitudinal studies are studies which are:

C – conducted at regular intervals over a long period of time

Q24 Secondary qualitative data, is data which

D – already exists such as diary entries

Q25 – Positivists question the reliability of participant observation because

B – they are difficult to replicate and so check the validity of any findings

Q26 – Ethnographic studies are

C- are seen as valid as the research is conducted in a natural setting

Q27 – Case studies usually involve the use of

C - interpretivist methods such as open-interviews or participant observations

Q28 – Triangulation is usually referred to as

D – methodological pluralism

Q29 – Longitudinal studies are studies which

B – collect data at regular intervals over a period of years

Q30 – There are three types of experiments sociologists can use

C – the laboratory, field and natural experiment

Q31 – Field experiments occur

B- in real-life conditions such as a school while trying to follow similar procedures to those found in any laboratory experiment

Q32 – One criticism of official statistics is they are sometimes

C – massaged by the state to avoid embarrassing the government of the day

ABOUT THE AUTHOR

The contents of the book have been written by sociologytwynham.com. For any other information or question you would like answering please contact us via the website. For other information on books in the series please visit the Revision page at sociologytwynham.com.